12.50
/1

Survivor Benefits of
Blue Collar Workers

Survivor Benefits of Blue Collar Workers

Melvin A. Glasser

Eugene L. Loren

Willard E. Solenberger

Michigan Health and Social Security
Research Institute, Inc.

Heath Lexington Books
D. C. Heath and Company
Lexington, Massachusetts

Contents

List of Tables

Preface

The survivors of deceased industrial workers face a wide variety of problems in their personal, social, and economic adjustments to the breadwinner's death, despite the growth of survivor benefits under Social Security and nongovernmental survivor protection programs. This study examines some of the central problems faced by the survivors of nearly 900 male workers employed in the automobile industry in the Detroit area who died in 1963 and 1965.

One of the principal objectives of this study is to permit survivor problems and their solutions to be viewed in the broadest perspective by those persons and agencies directly concerned with these problems—labor, management, private insurance carriers, and government. Such perspective is essential to the interrelated efforts required for the realization of increasingly effective measures to provide for the survivors of workers.

In the overview chapter immediately following, important implications of the study are summarized. These implications, based on the findings presented, represent the authors' judgments on important considerations deriving from the research. In the final analysis, however, the reader must draw his own conclusions from the data.

In conducting the study and preparing this report, the authors were affiliated with the Michigan Health and Social Security Research Institute, Inc., a nonprofit independent social research organization founded in the fall of 1963 by the International Union, United Automobile, Aerospace, and Agricultural Implement Workers of America (UAW). The Institute sponsored this study as one of a series of studies of the health, well-being, and social security of workers and their families.

The study was initially conceptualized by two of the authors, Willard E. Solenberger and Melvin A. Glasser. Thomas Barker, Ph.D., developed the questionnaires and worked with the National Opinion Research Center (NORC) in the collection of the field data prior to his departure from the Institute to take another position in June 1967. Eugene L. Loren carried principal responsibility for the project in the final stages. He developed the final tabulations and is the primary author of this report.

The study was financed principally by Grant Number 267 from the Cooperative Research and Demonstration Grants Program of the Social Security Administration of the U.S. Department of Health, Education, and Welfare. Financial support was also contributed by the UAW.

The study would not have been possible without the cooperation of a number of groups. Officials of the UAW contributed technical information and counsel at several crucial points. The automobile companies made available identifying information required for the selection of those included in the study—former employees of the General Motors Corporation, the Ford Motor Company, and Chrysler Corporation. The insurance carriers that underwrite the group life insurance contracts with these companies—Metropolitan Life Insurance Company, John Hancock Insurance Company, and Aetna Life Insurance Company—cooperated in assembling the required information. Finally, staff of the Social

Security Administration's Division of Program Research provided invaluable counsel at key stages in the development of the project.

Starting from the initial planning stages, Theodore Goldberg, Ph.D., Senior Medical Care Consultant; and Howard Young, F.S.A., Senior Actuary of the UAW Social Security Department staff; made valuable contributions as resource consultants in matters relating to insurance, other employee fringe benefit programs, and the United States Social Security Program.

Philip Booth, Lecturer in Social Work at the University of Michigan and formerly on the staff of the U.S. Department of Labor, acted as consulting director during the developmental phases of the study and reviewed the final manuscript. Paul B. Sheatsley, Director, Survey Research Service, National Opinion Research Center, wrote the initial drafts of Chapter 6, "Personal Implications of the Breadwinner's Death" and Appendix B, "Technical Notes on Methodology." He also served as a general consultant and contributed significantly to the design of the survey instruments and review of the final manuscript. The National Opinion Research Center assisted in the study design, conducted the field work, and processed the collected data. Carol Bowman of NORC was particularly helpful in the latter stage and aided in the overall analysis.

Finally, special appreciation must be expressed to the widows and other survivors who generously gave of their time in order to provide the information upon which this report is based. They share with us the hope that the data in this study will help make possible strengthened survivor protection programs.

To each and all who aided in the completion of the study, our sincere appreciation for generous and invaluable assistance is expressed. Any errors of commission or omission, of course, are the responsibility of the authors and the Research Institute alone.

The study represents, we believe, one of the first major efforts at developing reliable information in a social problem area of great concern to workers and their families—and indeed to all Americans. The findings have important social policy implications. They demonstrate, too, the need for continuing research further to augment the knowledge on which policy decisions can be made.

**Survivor Benefits of
Blue Collar Workers**

1

Overview

In a work-oriented society of high aspirations and living standards intimately linked to the receipt of regular and continuing income, it is of crucial importance to American workers to have adequate protection for their survivors in the event of death. The growth of social insurance programs accompanied by a vast expansion of private insurance suggests the magnitude of the commitment to this protection.

This report presents the findings of a study of a sample of the survivors of deceased blue-collar workers who had been actively employed in automobile manufacturing plants at the time of the worker's death. The study was primarily designed to investigate the overall adequacy and efficacy of lump sum death benefits and survivor income arrangements (both public and private) to the deceased workers' surviving families and other beneficiaries, if any. In addition, the social consequences of the death and the specific uses of the group insurance proceeds by the survivors—for the worker's funeral and other expenses—were also considered. Finally, general insights into survivor problems and programs are derived from the study findings and available data.

Aims and Methods

A sample of 873 male deaths of UAW represented auto workers employed by the General Motors Corporation, the Ford Motor Company, and the Chrysler Corporation in the Detroit Metropolitan area was analyzed with respect to the characteristics of the workers, as well as characteristics and adjustment experience of survivors. In several important respects, it is believed that these workers and the problems of their survivors are comparable to those of industrial workers and their survivors outside Detroit and the auto industry.

In generalizing to other groups and time periods, however, it must be recalled that the workers and survivors studied may have been better off financially than many of their peers not covered by the benefits described or not earning comparable wages. For example, as a group, the workers in the sample earned more than the national average money income for employed male civilians in the years studied.[a] Active auto workers and their survivors today (with generally

---

[a]*Statistical Abstract of the U.S.*, 1967, Table 479. Median money income is compared. In industrial terms (Table 480) the median work-related income of the sample studied exceeds that reported for male employed civilians by over $300 (1963) and over $500 (1965). If total family income is considered, the group studied fares relatively better (Table 472.) Thus, the gross money income firmly places the families studied in the middle class of all United States families.

higher wages and improved negotiated and public benefit coverages) are somewhat better off (than the group studied) in monetary though not necessarily in real income terms. The rise in the cost of living since 1966 has at least partially offset gains in monetary income.

The sample studied was drawn in approximately equal numbers from 1963 and 1965 deaths in order to analyze immediate and ongoing adjustment experience and problems. Personal interviews with the survivors took place in the spring of 1966, from 4 to 40 months after the worker's death. In both years, the sample included workers who left dependent beneficiaries and those who did not.

Extensive information on the worker's background, the predeath and postdeath financial situation and the survivor's adjustment experience was obtained for those workers leaving dependent survivors (Long Form Questionnaire). Since similarly detailed information was not readily obtainable from those survivors who had not been dependent on the worker, only major worker demographic characteristics and information regarding the worker's funeral and other estate settlement expenses were obtained from the respondents (Short Form Questionnaire).

Though the analysis of the dependent survivor's experience was based on the financial and other data obtained, it is recognized that merely comparing death benefits and expenses understates the true loss resulting from the worker's death. It is practically impossible, for example, to measure the costs of normal household maintenance—once a responsibility of the husband—that must be handled in different ways, often at significant expense, after the death of the wage earner.

The major hypotheses examined in the study may be summarized as follows: The existing survivor benefits programs (public and private combined) are adequate to meet the immediate financial adjustment needs of the survivors, following the death of the worker, but are inadequate to meet the ongoing financial needs of this group.

A further hypothesis—that lump sum benefits, above some not yet determined level, had little positive value as compared with monthly income benefits—was part of the initial study design. However, this hypothesis could not be adequately investigated. Insufficient numbers of survivors elected to receive available life insurance as monthly income.

The test of the immediate adequacy of nongovernmental benefits was the amount of lump sum group life insurance proceeds compared to the immediate adjustment costs facing survivors, that is, funeral costs, medical bills, and estate administration costs. In making this test, consideration was also given to assets and debts left by deceased workers.

To evaluate the ongoing adequacy of all types of survivor benefits, a broader measure was obtained. The annualized income of the survivors studied, as reported at the time of the interview, was compared to a family budget standard adopted for the purposes of this study—the Detroit City Worker's Family Budget (DCWFB).[b]

For 1965 survivors, the period of time following the worker's death (4-16 months) was too brief to permit anything but a preliminary evaluation of the adequacy of the available resources to meet ongoing financial requirements. For 1963 survivors, however, use of the DCWFB standard provided an approximate measure of such adequacy from a somewhat longer run standpoint.

The still relatively brief elapsed time since the worker's death limits the use of the DCWFB as a true measure of long run adequacy for the survivors studied. For example, to the extent that duration and amount of public and private benefits vary overtime, or earnings opportunities develop or are lost, or the number of dependents changes, actual long run adequacy can only be inferred with additional assumptions. Some of the principal findings of this study are listed below (this material is expanded throughout the rest of the book).

Characteristics of Workers and Survivors

a. Approximately six out of seven workers left the proceeds of their negotiated group life insurance to dependent survivors. In over 90% of these cases, the widow was the beneficiary. The one worker in seven who did not leave dependent survivors, left his group insurance proceeds to relatives in all but 8% of the cases studied.

b. The typical deceased auto worker was 56 years old at the time of his death and his wife was nearly 52. At the time of his death, the typical worker had been employed by his last employer for over 20 years.

c. Heart disease was the largest single cause of death. In nine out of ten deaths, an illness (as distinguished from an accident) was the cause.

d. The typical surviving unit was headed by a widow. The widow alone survived in 45% of the cases involving dependent survivors. In one out of five surviving units (20%) one additional dependent survived with the widow; while in 13% of the units, a widow and two additional dependents survived. In fewer than 21% of the surviving units did more than two dependents survive the worker.

e. Childless widows 45-50 years old were about 75% of all such widows under 50 years of age.

---

[b]As indicated in Chapter 2, the DCWFB standard is a conservative measure in several important respects. For example, the cost of personal taxes, if any, are omitted from the basic standard against which income is compared. Moreover, a direct BLS estimate for 1966 (released too late for use in this study) when reduced to reflect 1965 prices, shows the standard used in the study to be approximately 25% below the 1966 estimate of a modest standard of living. Use of the adjusted 1966 budget would show more survivors significantly further below the DCWFB standard. A discussion of the DCWFB as a measure of adequacy is included in Chapter 2 and Appendix B.

4

f. In 47% of the dependent surviving units, there were children under the age of 20. Of these, there were children under the age of 9 in 6% of the units; between 9 and 13 in 4%; and in 37% of the surviving families, the youngest child was between 13 and 20.

g. The great majority of widows (70%) were not working at the time of their husband's death. Most widows, however, had had some work experience. Typical education included some high school, though not graduation.

Resources Created by the Worker's Death

a. Benefits available to the widow and other survivors derived from the worker's group life insurance, private life insurance and Social Security. The majority of the workers studied had private insurance that supplemented their negotiated group coverage.

b. Median amount of lump sum resources created by the worker's death was $7330 (1963) and $8270 (1965). This included group insurance (median—$6660 - 1963; $7050 - 1965) as well as the Social Security Lump Sum Death Payment (maximum $255) and private insurance coverage (median for those covered - $1110 - 1963; $1370 - 1965).

c. As an indication of skewness of the above distribution, 99% of the 1963 survivors and 97% of the 1965 survivors had total insurance proceeds from the worker's death exceeding $3000. More than 96% of both years' survivors had such proceeds created in excess of $5000.

d. Approximately half of the dependent surviving units had little or no net assets (between $1000 debt and $1000 assets) to supplement survivor benefits or work income or as potential charges against such income.

Immediate Death Related Expenses

a. Fewer than 25% of the survivors (both years) reported unpaid health care charges due for the care of the deceased worker in excess of $100. Catastrophic health care charges due (that is, greater than $1000) were experienced by less than 1% of the survivors. More than a third of the survivors reported no outstanding bills in this category.

b. Median immediate death related expenses (exclusive of providing for outstanding debts) was $1575 (1963) and $1590 (1965). For both years combined, only 6% of the survivors reported such expenses in excess of $3000.

c. If the total of immediate death related expenses is deducted from total lump sum resources created by the death, hypothetical median amounts of $6340 (1963) and $7060 (1965) are potentially available to meet living expenses. The shortfall of income as compared to the budget standard used (DCWFB) required survivors to draw down their assets. This finding is confirmed below.

d. Based on interest income reported, it is apparent that few survivors had significant monetary assets upon which they could draw to supplement income. In response to a direct question regarding group life insurance proceeds remaining at the time of interview, 53% of those failing to meet the DCWFB adequacy standard by $500 or more reported less than $2000 of such proceeds which might be used to meet this deficiency.

e. Median group life insurance proceeds reported as actually still available were $1760 (1963 survivors) and $4080 (1965 survivors). The primary difference between the groups is the adjustment period covered. Though data on proceeds retained from sources other than group life insurance are not available, it appears to the researchers that the amount of unspent group life insurance money at the time of interview (perhaps supplemented by nongroup life proceeds) would in all probability be exhausted in a relatively short period if applied toward meeting the family income deficiencies (against the DCWFB standard) reported below.

Ongoing Adjustment

a. Thirty-five percent of the dependent survivors of workers who died in 1965 fell more than $500 below the DCWFB standard.[c] While many widows in this group had not yet begun to work to supplement income, it is noted that 88% of the 1965 survivors included the Transition Survivor Income Benefit[d] in their reported income.

b. A longer ongoing period was evaluated for 1963 survivors. None in this group were receiving the Transition Benefit. However, a higher percentage of these widows were working to supplement income and a greater percentage of the dependents had married or otherwise left home. For the group of 1963 survivors (excluding those remarried), 48% fell below the adjusted DCWFB standard by $500 or more.

c. Thirty-four percent of the 1963 dependent survivors and 46% of the 1965 group of survivors reported incomes which exceeded the DCWFB standard by $500 or more.

d. Fewer than 10% of the nonremarried widows reported children under 13 years of age. Though nearly half of the 1965 families with children under this age had incomes more than $500 greater than the DCWFB standard, fewer than 10% of such 1963 families met the corresponding measure.

e. Size of family, as such, was not important as a variable explaining adjustment as measured on the DCWFB scale.

---

[c]An income was defined as meeting the DCWFB standard if it was within $500 of the stated DCWFB budget value.

[d]This benefit provided in the union-management collective bargaining agreements was $100 per month in 1963 and in 1965 and was payable to specified dependent survivors for up to two years following the wage earner's death. See Chapter 2 for a detailed description.

f. Despite the relative suddenness of the worker's death, survivors of accidental death victims fared somewhat better than other survivors as measured on the DCWFB scale. Their average age was younger than that of other survivors. The corresponding work and remarriage potential, in addition to the additional death benefit (at General Motors and Ford an accidental death benefit of 50% of the principal amount of group life insurance was payable to workers dying as the result of an accident), apparently was sufficient to boost the income of survivors of accidental death victims above the average of all survivors.

g. As expected, widows working full time fared better with respect to DCWFB score than other widows. Still, of the 1963 deaths, 30% of those working full time scored only at the DCWFB level or below. Part time working widows fared inconsistently though somewhat better than those widows who did not work. Fewer than 12% of those widows who did not work exceeded the DCWFB standard.[e]

h. Again, as expected, the number of working dependents tended to increase a family's DCWFB score. Among survivors of 1963 decedents, 76% of the family units without working dependents scored below the DCWFB standard. For the same group, 22% of those with two or more working dependents failed to meet this standard. A similar relation exists among the 1965 survivors.

i. Receipt of Social Security benefits was not sufficient for many of the families studied to assure adequacy of income. For survivors of the 1963 deaths, for example, 51% of those receiving Social Security benefits failed to meet the DCWFB standard by more than $500. This is contrasted with 38% of those without such benefits that failed to meet this standard. Only a fourth of the 1965 decedents receiving Social Security failed to meet the DCWFB income standard used. In part, the difference between the two years is a reflection of the adjustment time considered and the differences in the extent to which the widows and dependents involved were working. The above is consistent with the finding regarding relative inadequacy of income as measured by DCWFB standard and the ages of surviving dependent children. It must be recalled that work earnings, beyond a stated variable amount, disqualify a beneficiary from Social Security benefits. Moreover, Social Security recipients include a disproportionate share of the oldest and youngest widows. How far short of its goals the Social Security survivor benefit program is falling is apparent, however, if when, combined with one of the better nongovernmental programs, it still fails to meet the minimum budgetary needs for one quarter to one half of the recipients.

j. Family financial resources available at the worker's death (savings, securities, property, and business value) to supplement survivor benefits and other

---

[e]It must be remembered that the DCWFB score is a particularly conservative measure for working widows as, for example, the cost of personal taxes is omitted from this budget standard. Thus, even though working, many of the 1963 widows and a significant group of the 1965 widows were not able to achieve an income sufficient to be classed as modest but adequate by the Bureau of Labor Statistics.

income are generally not significant. Of the survivors of 1963 decedents, 69% reported under $2000 in such resources. Of the 1965 survivors, 62% reported under $2000 in total financial resources. When debts are considered the net resources available to supplement reported incomes are apparently even less likely sources that might overcome the reported deficiencies in income.

k. More than one out of four family units of the 1963 group of survivors reported changing their residence after the worker's death. While this is probably not significant in comparison with the experience of other workers, the reasons reported for moving are of interest. Financial reasons, including help with caring for children while the mother worked, were most often cited by movers. Other living expenses were reduced by more than one out of four of the survivor units.

l. An indirect finding of the study is the absence of reported receipt of public welfare funds. Though no specific question was asked about welfare income, as such, respondents were asked to report all sources of income. Less than 1% of the respondents reported public assistance as a source of funds. The presence of cash resources would, in most cases, exclude the survivors studied from the receipt of public welfare grants. Moreover, even the low income reported by many survivors generally exceeds welfare standards in the Detroit area.

Uses of Group Insurance Proceeds

a. The median cost of auto worker funerals ($1563 - 1963) exceeded the highest estimate (reported by Ruth Harmer) of the cost of funerals with the trimmings for that year ($1461) and was well above the national average cost ($988). Though the auto worker average figure excludes infant and indigent funerals included in the national average, it is still higher than the maximum estimates reported. If it is true that knowledge by the undertakers of available life insurance is a factor in the selection and sale of given funeral arrangements, the relatively large amount available to auto worker survivors may in part account for this relatively high figure.

b. Other reported uses of group life insurance proceeds varied with the stage of adjustment, with 1965 survivors more frequently reporting saving at least part of the group insurance proceeds. Approximately three-quarters of the 1963 survivors and half of the 1965 survivors reported that they were using at least part of their group insurance proceeds for current consumption purposes.

Personal Impact of the Breadwinner's Death

a. As expected, remarriage and remarriage plans are strongly related to the widow's age and size of family. Though only 8% of 1963 widow survivors had remarried at the time of interview, more than 20% of such survivors with children under age nine had remarried.

b. Approximately 20% of the survivors reported use of nonfamily sources of financial advice following the death of the worker. Though most reported satisfaction with such advice, more than one-fifth reported that they should have sought alternative sources, generally a lawyer.

c. Group activity of the widows interviewed declined appreciably following the deaths of their husbands.

d. The percentage of children doing not so well in school as before their father's death doubled for the 1963 survivors and more than tripled for the 1965 group.

Assessing the Findings

In assessing all of the above findings, it should be recognized that the distinction between immediate and ongoing expenses, as well as the DCWFB and other measures of adequacy, are artificial constructs developed to facilitate the measurement and analysis of this study. While imperfect, such devices were used conservatively within the limits attributed to them. They reveal important aspects of the problems and death induced adjustments of the survivors of industrial workers.

In summary, the immediate adequacy measure (comparing death generated lump sum resources and expenses) indicates the survivor's general ability to meet those expenses most directly related to the worker's death. In the establishment of an ongoing budget standard, the measure used (DCWFB) implicitly assumes that the immediate expenses have been met. Although necessarily less than exact, the DCWFB is believed to be a generally conservative indicator of the economic adjustment problems of survivors.

Thus, the indicated deficiencies in financial resources for the group studied may actually understate their longer range adjustment problems. For example, life insurance benefits, even if taken in monthly installments, are fixed in amount and of limited duration. The $100 per month Transition Benefit (payable to specified dependent survivors in 1965 and with modification since) is payable for only two years. While, following receipt of a Transition Benefit, most of the 1965 widows qualify by age (over age 50 at the worker's death) for a Bridge Benefit of $100 per month, this is not payable if a mother's benefit (under Social Security) is being received and ceases in any case at age 62.

Moreover, while except for Social Security (which may be adjusted through legislation) the benefits of survivors of active employees have generally been fixed by the collective bargaining agreement in effect at the time of the worker's death,[f] the cost and standard of living obviously are not fixed. In addition,1963

---

[f]The generalization was not adhered to in 1967, when company paid health insurance for survivors of deceased UAW Big Three (and other auto industry) employees, either retired or eligible to retire, was negotiated to be applicable to pre-1967 deaths. Pension benefits are a general exception.

through 1966 were good years for auto workers and the economy. The study data reflect this as well as the fact that the years preceding the worker's death had been relatively good ones also. Given the infrequency of general price reductions, it is felt that should the economy or the auto industry fall on harder times the picture might be considerably worse (possibly as the result of less net assets and earnings by secondary wage earners prior to the worker's death) despite the assured nature of the benefits themselves.

In generalizing beyond the auto industry to groups with lesser income or survivor and related benefits, the above must be recognized. For groups with greater incomes or more comprehensive survivor and related benefits, rising costs and standards of living must similarly be recognized. In both cases, projections of future income and benefits are extremely hazardous. However, given the age and earning background of most of the widow survivors covered in this study, earnings opportunities may be generally expected to decline with advancing age.

Policy Implications

In interpreting the study findings, judgment regarding survivor benefit adequacy is based on consideration of immediate and ongoing survivor needs. On this basis, it can be seen that despite individual efforts at self-help (for example, widows and other dependents working) and the existence of public and private survivor benefit programs based on right, a substantial number of survivors are failing to meet what has been defined as a modest but adequate standard of living. Even the existence of variable amounts of residual lump sum resources (not accurately ascertainable), if applied to this deficiency, probably would not alter the above picture very much or for a very long period.

Toward meeting the apparent income deficiency, improvements in Social Security would have the most widespread effect. In addition, the following observations are worth considering in association with future developments and modifications in survivor benefit programs.

1. The existing combination of public and private institutional arrangements for survivor protection, even for the relatively advantaged auto workers studied and probably more so for other wage earner groups, needs to be augmented if the ongoing economic problems faced by survivors are to be met adequately.
2. The researchers were unable to examine directly the tentative hypothesis that lump sum payments of life insurance above a specified amount or range of amounts tend to be disfunctional in meeting the ongoing adjustment needs of survivors. Of some relevance to this hypothesis, however, was the finding that lump sums paid to dependent survivors in the study sample appear to have exceeded, in most cases by a considerable margin, immediate adjustment expenses. In addition, subsequent income provisions for a substantial number of widows were deficient, as measured by the DCWFB. These factors suggest that more attention needs to be given to the institutional arrangements

(public and private) for ongoing income benefits than to the provision of lump sum benefits as such.

3. Independent of benefit level and structure, the study indicates the need for more readily available and possibly more effective financial counselling services as an aid to surviving families in maximizing the utility of available survivor protection.

Choosing among possible insurance payment options and between these and alternative applications of insurance proceeds in the light of the total family situation are examples of areas in which such counselling services might contribute to a more effective functioning of benefits.

As indicated above, approximately half of the survivor units reported virtually no net assets upon which they could draw to supplement their incomes. Such survivors have particular need for counselling that might also enable them to obtain suitable training or employment to augment income. In addition, several of the survivor benefits reported as income are essentially short term in nature (for example, the Transition Benefit is paid for not more than 24 months). Counselling can anticipate future necessary adjustments and, as such, has long-term value.

4. A current trend in group life insurance underwriting toward the provision of monthly survivor income benefits (for example, the UAW-negotiated Transition and Bridge benefit coverages) to those with the greatest presumptive need is evidence of current interest in fresh approaches to survivor protection. Further research is needed to assess adequately the social utility and premium cost savings to be achieved from such developments. This study offers some direct support, however, to the thesis underlying this trend—that objective bases can be established for discriminating between classes of potential survivor beneficiaries. Such discrimination may be desired in order to direct benefits to specific categories of beneficiaries likely to be in greatest need of assured ongoing income, while at the same time retaining the basic insurance principle of payment as a matter of right, without a means test.

5. Given the costs involved and the generally recognized trauma associated with death, the study findings suggest that greater attention to death and burial preplanning and counselling might be useful. Death is an unpleasant subject, at best, however, advance knowledge of some of the costs and problems associated with it may help the survivor avoid some of the more obvious pitfalls that might otherwise be present. Unions or cooperatives might consider demonstration projects to further explore dignified means of burial at reasonable costs. No one expects the widow to shop for funerals. The availability of controlled plans that are known to workers and survivors, however, would provide an important alternative to the commericial approaches now most widely used. In any case, it is apparent that the Social Security lump sum death payment (maximum $255) is nowhere near adequate to cover burial or the other lump sum costs associated with death.

6. The study findings also indicate the need for improved and expanded (non-financial) counselling resources to aid the families and particularly the

children of recently deceased workers. The emotional adjustment problems of survivors are widely acknowledged. Still, public resources to cope with such problems are apparently scarce and inconsistently utilized. Education is an important area where a problem exists and more effective counselling is obviously required.

7. Though beyond the immediate scope of the present study, such programs as a guaranteed annual income or family allowance, by whatever means determined, would obviously aid many survivors. The extent to which such provisions would have altered the picture presented in this study and would resolve the problems highlighted (for these and other survivors), would depend on the nature and form of the provision adopted.

2

Background, Aims, and Methodology

American society, in common with most industrial societies, attempts to provide at least a degree of economic protection for the survivors of wage earners through a multitude of devices, with varying degrees of public and private involvement. Both public and private devices include assistance and protection based on concepts of right and need. In the private realm, individual and group efforts toward survivor protection have been utilized. In the public realm, varying degrees of protection are available through both the federal, state and local governments.

At the federal level, aged widows and widowed mothers and their dependent children, may be eligible for survivor benefits as a matter of right under Title II of the Social Security Act, the Railroad Retirement Act, Veteran's Administration programs, and miscellaneous provisions applicable to governmental employees. In 1965, for example, it was estimated that 4.7 million beneficiaries were drawing $4 billion in survivor benefits under Old Age, Survivors, Disability, and Health Insurance—an increase of nearly fifteenfold over the $277 million paid out under this program in 1950.[a] It has been estimated further that 80% of widow-child families were receiving benefits under this program in 1962.[1]

At the state level, varying degrees of protection for surviving widows and families are provided under Workmen's Compensation laws covering deaths resulting from job related illness and accidents. It is estimated that in 1965, $145 million was paid in monthly benefits to survivors entitled to benefits as a result of a death covered by Workmen's Compensation programs.[2] This is an increase of nearly 300% over the $55 million paid out under such programs in 1950.

Survivor economic protection is available in the private sector through group and individual insurance arrangements and company pension plans with survivor benefits. In 1960, approximately 82% of United States males had some form of life insurance, including 39% who had group life insurance coverage. Death payments from these life insurance policies exceeded $5.2 billion in 1966. The average value of all insurance coverage for those covered in 1960 was $9690. For those with group insurance, the average policy coverage was $6320.[3]

---

[a]*Social Security Bulletin,* Annual Statistical Supplement, 1965, Table 7 (the latest data presently available). This increase and the increase in Workmen's Compensation benefits noted in the following paragraph reflect increases in both coverage and benefit amounts. These and other data describing private and public survivor benefit programs are illustrative of the magnitudes involved. Given the variability of the periods for which comparable data are available, no attempt is made to present a complete and current picture of survivor protection programs.

Survivors of workers who are employed in the automobile industry are eligible for survivor benefits (group insurance, health and pension benefits) provided through collective bargaining which obligates the employer to provide a stated benefit on a contractual basis. In general, these plans are considered to be among the most comprehensive coverages available to industrial workers. In addition, auto workers (and their families) are protected by negotiated programs of broad scale health insurance benefits. Details of these plans as they applied to the 1963 and 1965 survivors are provided in this chapter.

The design of all the above survivor benefit programs implicitly recognizes a common function: that is, the provision of monetary or equivalent resources to survivors following a wage earner's death in order to minimize personal hardship and dependency on others. These resources are available as a matter of right, as a result of public or private programs (the latter involving either individual, or employment related, or other group arrangements). As indicated above, the major forms of survivor benefits are monthly income payments and minimal lump sum death benefits under Title II of the Social Security Act and other similar governmental programs, individual and group life insurance proceeds (generally lump sum), and survivor pensions.

In addition to the above survivor benefit programs based on right, survivors may also draw on general benefit programs, such as Aid to Dependent Children (ADC) and Public Assistance, based on varying tests of need. Traditionally, society has recognized and accepted certain responsibilities to provide for those it defines to be in need. At the same time, recognition has been given to the desirability of a substantial element of private voluntary efforts, in conjunction with the operation of public programs. The specific means of providing for those in need (that is, the mix of public and private activities) as well as the degree of relief provided, has changed through time.[4]

Concern for the problems of survivors, however, also reflects changing social attitudes and public policies. In evaluating the degree of public and private responsibility for those in need, society must continually examine such questions as:

1. What levels of income are required to maintain an acceptable standard of living?
2. What is the degree of individual responsibility to attain such levels of income?
3. What is the best way to carry out the accepted level of public responsibility?
4. Are the individual's social needs as distinct from economic needs parts of the same public problem?

This study cannot explicitly answer the above questions. It does, however, shed light on some of the problems underlying these questions. It does so by focusing on these problems as they apply to a group of survivors of industrial workers, who, as a consequence of a largely unpredictable event—the death of a primary breadwinner—find themselves in circumstances potentially requiring help from society if a reasonable standard of living is to be maintained.

In examining the adjustment problems faced by a sample of these survivors, this report considers the nature of their needs; the ways in which they and society presently attempt to meet these needs; and ways in which their ability to meet their needs might be improved.

Aims and Hypotheses

From the beginning, the researchers recognized the existence of an apparent paradox: while public and private provisions for aiding survivors have expanded in scope, resulting in the distribution of nearly 13 billions of dollars in survivor benefits under Social Security and private individual and group insurance benefits in 1967, knowledge of these benefits, their uses and adequacy, has not grown accordingly. Thus, today, very little is known about the answers to such questions as:

1. Who actually receives survivor benefits?
2. How is survivor benefit income used?
3. What are the other income sources and other resources of workers and their survivors?
4. What are the major social adjustment problems of dependent survivors?

As suggested above, this investigation attempts to contribute to the existing knowledge of survivor benefits by focusing on only one group of survivors; the survivors of certain blue-collar workers who were formerly employed in the automobile industry. In the course of the investigation, the above and related questions have been considered. With the Detroit Metropolitan area as the geographic base, the investigation explored the social and economic consequences of the loss to the family of its primary source of financial support.

Specific Aims

The specific aims of the study were to

1. describe the economic consequences of the worker's death on the survivors;
2. describe the utilization of survivor benefits;
3. determine if there are differences in uses and effectiveness of lump sum proceeds of insurance policies, as compared to continuing income payment arrangements under group insurance;
4. determine what social adjustments the surviving families make following the worker's death; and
5. identify and evaluate any professional or other counselling resources utilized by survivors.

In the course of the study, efforts to examine data on survivors choosing to receive their life insurance proceeds in the form of monthly installments were modified in view of findings indicating the limited election of such monthly installment income options.

In meeting these aims, the following broad aspects of survivor experience were examined specifically:

1. the characteristics of deceased workers. In order to evaluate the adequacy of survivor benefits, a base line was established to describe the family's prefatality circumstances. Worker and family characteristics are considered in Chapter 3, "Characteristics of Workers and Survivors";
2. the overall adequacy of the survivor benefit programs—including the efficacy of the present combination of lump sum and monthly income benefits—as provided through Social Security, group and individual private insurance and other mechanisms. This material is considered in Chapters 4 and 5, "Economic Impact of the Breadwinner's Death," and "Utilization of Life Insurance Proceeds";
3. the financial obligations incurred prior to and immediately following the worker's death relative to the adequacy of survivor benefits received—a special aspect of the problem of overall adequacy. With today's emphasis on consumer credit and installment purchases, the impact of debt is of particular significance. This topic is considered in Chapters 4 and 5, also.
4. the social and personal problems of survivors and the possible need for social and financial counseling services, identifying the reported sources of the services utilized. In view of the survivors sudden acquisition of new financial resources and new responsibilities, the availability of counseling is increasingly significant and is considered in Chapter 6, "Personal Implications of the Breadwinner's Death."

Major Hypotheses

The research methodology was designed to examine the following major hypotheses:

Hypothesis 1. The existing survivor benefits programs, considered in the aggregate, are adequate to meet the *immediate* financial adjustment needs of survivors following the death of the worker.

Hypothesis 2. The existing survivor benefits programs, considered in the aggregate, are inadequate (in many cases) to meet the *ongoing* financial needs of survivors in the years following the death of the worker.

Hypothesis 3. Lump sum settlements, above a yet undetermined minimum amount, as opposed to regular monthly payments made available to survivors by life insurance and other programs, may actually provide a social and economic service of little real value to workers' survivors.

Direct efforts to evaluate monthly income in contrast to lump sum benefits were omitted early in the course of the study. The study revealed that, consistent with privately reported insurance industry experience, 2% of the survivors elected the monthly installment income settlement option under the group insurance plan. In addition, the differing characteristics of those with and without Social Security benefits, for example, age and work characteristics, make direct comparisons involving such monthly income invalid. Finally, for the 1965 group, virtually all survivors had some form of monthly income, that is, Transition Benefits, for a two-year period.

Thus, it was impossible to test the third hypothesis or the corresponding aim. Indirect evidence on this question is presented in Chapters 4 and 5.

The immediate financial adjustment needs are defined as the financial resources survivors require to meet the immediate adjustment costs[b] associated with a worker's death. The criterion for establishing the adequacy or inadequacy of the benefit program, under Hypothesis 1, is the ability of the insurance benefits to meet these costs for the surviving family units studied.

Only widow-headed family units were studied relative to Hypothesis 2. Ongoing was considered to include a period of time at the conclusion of which the widow remarried and could no longer be assumed to be dependent on her income as a survivor; otherwise there was no identifiable termination.

Because of the limited time interval between the death of the worker and the time of interview of the survivors (a maximum of 40 months), it is not possible to present an extensive analysis bearing on the question of the true ongoing long-term financial adjustments of many surviving units. Based on certain stipulated assumptions, however, some indications of these ongoing adjustment problems of survivors are presented.

To establish criteria to measure the adequacy of the total survivor benefit provisions in meeting ongoing needs, a comparison was made of the family's postfatality income and a standard budget. A standard, which is referred to as "The Detroit City Worker's Family Budget"(DCWFB), has been constructed for this study. It provides a measure of the cost of maintaining the individual family unit at a level of living (in 1966) comparable to that described as modest but adequate in 1959.[c] This standard is based on an adaptation of the City Worker's

---

[b]In the popular language of the insurance industry the initial adjustment costs are variously referred to as cleanup funds, Probate Funds or estate clearance funds. They consist of (1) hospital, doctors, and similar bills incident to the last illness; (2) burial expenses, including funeral costs, cemetery lot, and marker; (3) personal obligations, including unpaid notes, personal loans, installment payments, and other unsatisfied accounts; (4) unpaid pledges, whether or not they are legally binding obligations; (5) cost of estate administration, including executor's or administrator's fees, appraisers' fees, legal fees, and court costs; and (6) estate, inheritance, income, and property taxes. This is the definition adhered to in the present study, except as noted.

[c]Helen H. Lamale and Margaret S. Stotz report that the City Worker's Family Budget (CWFB on which the DCWFB was based) was designed to "estimate the dollar amount

Family Budget (CWFB) originally developed by the Bureau of Labor Statistics in 1946-47,[d] and subsequently updated to 1959. The budget includes allowances for day-to-day living expenses such as food, housing, clothing, and medical care.

In interpreting the survivor income reported in comparison to the DCWFB standard, it is recognized that this standard is an imperfect one.

As much of the survivor's postfatality income is tax free, and most widows were not found to be working, such variables as financial requirements for personal taxes, social security deductions, life insurance, and occupational expenses, were excluded in comparing reported income with the DCWFB standard. This exclusion is one reason that leads the authors to conclude that the DCWFB standard derived is essentially conservative, that is, leads to an overstatement of the numbers regarded as having a modest but adequate income.

The conservative nature of the standard used is further indicated by its assumption of a housing cost that derives from rental of a standard five room home or apartment. Nearly four out of five of the workers (like most Detroit residents) and two out of three surviving units were reported as owning their own homes.

By comparing total family income and the modest DCWFB standard, adjusted as indicated, a measure of the surplus or deficit from a modest but adequate standard of living is obtained. The DCWFB used for 1966 is included in Appendix A, "Technical Notes on Methodology." A further discussion and comparison to other budgets is also included.

---

required to maintain such a family (4 persons, consisting of an employed husband, wife not employed outside the home, and two children) at a level of adequate living, according to prevailing standards of what is needed for health, efficiency, the nurture of children, and for participation in the social and community activities . . ." "The Interim City Worker's Family Budget," *Monthly Labor Review*, (August, 1960) p. 785.

[d]The CWFB was adjusted for this analysis by eliminating the computations for the husband and making allowances for more dependents. It was updated to 1966 by calculating changes in the Detroit Consumer Price Index and applying these changes to the annual cost of the Detroit CWFB 1959 estimates in accordance with the scale of equivalent income. For further discussion of the CWFB and the scale of equivalent income see "Technical Notes: Estimating Equivalent Incomes on Budget Costs by Family Types," Marsha Froeder, *Monthly Labor Review*, (November, 1960) pp. 1197-1200. In late 1967, a revised budget standard was released by the Bureau of Labor Statistics. This standard was available too late for inclusion in the present analysis. However, it represents a significantly higher cost and standard of living. Helen Lamale, Division of Living Conditions Studies, Bureau of Labor Statistics, and Mollie Orshansky, Division of Research and Statistics, Social Security Administration assisted in the development of the DCWFB used in this study. Though fully recognizing the limits of this measure, they agreed that it combined several important adequacy variables in one measure and as such was potentially valuable. (For additional discussion of the DCWFB see Appendix A.)

Summary of Methodology

The basic design of the study, planned in 1965 for interviewing in 1966, called for personal interviews with the survivors of deceased male (only) auto workers, focusing on the economic and social consequences of the worker's death and the uses to which the survivors' benefits were put. For purposes of basic comparability of benefits as well as economy and efficiency, the investigation was restricted, as already noted, to survivors of UAW represented deceased employees of the "Big Three" auto companies (General Motors, Ford, Chrysler) who had lived in the Detroit area.

The Samples

The design further called for two separate samples of survivor families, distinguished by the length of time that had elapsed since the fatality. There was interest in the immediate consequences of the fatality and in the experiences of survivors who were still in the process of adjusting to their new situation. For this purpose, 1965, the latest full year for which worker mortality data were available, was selected.

There was also interest in the ongoing adjustment of the worker's family following immediate postdeath adjustments. This objective required a study of deaths occurring at least two or three years prior to the interviewing. In selecting deaths from the year 1963 for the study of ongoing adjustment, any later year was rejected as allowing too short a time span beyond immediate adjustment to be significant. Moreover, auto negotiations occurred in the final quarter of 1964 and the pattern of negotiated survivor benefits was changed. The selection of an earlier year (1962) would have increased the danger of unreliable and selective recall on the part of the respondents and would also have increased the difficulty of locating survivors. Given the above factors, 1963 was chosen.

While it has originally been planned to sample all deaths during the selected years, the decision was made, following the sample pretest in the field, to restrict the study to the survivors of males. Females accounted for only 8% of auto worker deaths during the two years, too small a segment to justify separate analysis; yet they could scarcely be lumped with the other cases since their survivors usually included employed husbands. Given the limited budget for interviews, the efficiency of the sample was thus improved by omitting females.

In about one case in six, the deceased auto worker left no dependent survivors. Beneficiaries in such cases were adult children, parents, brothers or sisters, other relatives, or perhaps friends. As these survivors were self-supporting and usually resided in a different household, much of the questionnaire was irrelevant or inappropriate to their situation. Accordingly, an abbreviated Short Form questionnaire was developed for these respondents, which inquired only into immediate postdeath and burial expenses and amount of insurance received.

Interviewing was conducted in the early spring of 1966, so that the death investigated for the 1965 group of survivors had occurred from four to sixteen months earlier. For the 1963 group, the death had occurred from 28 to 40 months earlier.

As indicated above, for each year studied, the survivor-beneficiaries were grouped according to whether they had been dependent on the deceased wage earner. Dependency was defined to include a wife or any other survivor who had received more than half of his support from the wage earner. Dependent survivors were interviewed in detail on a Long Form (L.F.) questionnaire. As mentioned, nondependent survivors were questioned in less detail on a Short Form (S.F) questionnaire.

Thus, while important data on the worker and burial expenses are available for both groups, not all information is available for all workers or beneficiaries. Still, comparisons of workers leaving dependent and nondependent beneficiaries may be made, along with important comparisons of these beneficiaries.

Tabular presentations use the Dependent (Dep.) and NonDependent (Non-Dep.) designations. These designations refer to the presence or absence of dependent beneficiaries and correspond to the Long Form or Short Form questionnaire used to interview the survivors.

Copies of the questionnaires used are included in Appendix C. Appendix B includes a detailed summary of the DCWFB (including values), the methodology used, and a table of Percentage Sampling Errors, for use in interpreting the data presented. Errors of estimate for means and medians are also discussed.

General Applicability of Study

In assessing the generalizability of these findings to other times, other places, and other survivor groups, it should be recognized that the selected years were generally prosperous ones for the auto companies and for the United States as a whole, and that the population interviewed was restricted to survivors of workers employed by three of our largest corporations and residing in and around the Detroit metropolitan area.

Moreover, improvements have occurred in auto worker survivor benefits since the study year 1966. In the 1967 negotiations, for example, maximum group life insurance amounts were increased to reflect higher wage levels, and Bridge and Transition Survivor Income benefits (for specified categories of survivors) were also raised. These elements of survivor protection are explained more fully in the next section. In addition to changes in the negotiated insurance program, Social Security benefit levels were increased in 1968.

While it is impossible to specify, it is argued that this study's findings, subject (at times) to predictable modification for the group considered, retain a significant degree of generalized applicability beyond the period, the sample, and the auto industry. In generalizing these findings to other groups, certain variable factors at times offset each other. In other instances, the direction of variation may be predicted according to basic differences, such as income in the groups compared.

An example of potentially offsetting factors involves price and benefit movements. Thus, while public and private benefit levels have increased since 1966, so has the cost of living. The fact that family living costs in the Detroit area are just under the United States urban average should be recognized in generalizing the findings to other urban groups.[5]

Thus, given the relatively high levels of insurance benefits and incomes of auto workers, it is not unreasonable to estimate that as a group, survivors of other industrial workers fare no better and many generally fare worse.[e]

Auto Worker Survivor Benefits

Both employers and employees accept group life insurance as a significant and valuable fringe benefit. (For the Big Three, alone, for example, almost $55 million was spent in 1967 on group life insurance premiums.) As such, group life insurance may be viewed realistically as an important element of total employee compensation. Thus, the worker and his employer have a collective interest in both the cost and effectiveness of insurance arrangements. They also share a concern that the protection purchased be fully understood by employees and his survivors.

Generally, negotiated employee benefit programs among all of the Big Three automobile manufacturers have been comparable in recent years. Though there were minor variations in provision, these are not considered significant in relation to this study.[6] Up to the 1964 auto negotiations, survivor protection had traditionally been obtained through group life insurance which provided a stated lump sum payable to an employee's named beneficiary, who could elect to receive this amount in monthly installments, but in fact rarely did so.

The survivor protection provisions in force under the auto insurance programs prior to the 1964 settlements (applicable to survivors of the 1963 group of decedents) included the following major elements:

1. a schedule of wage related group life insurance in amounts ranging from $5,500 to $10,500;
2. additional protection, 50% of the above amounts were available (except at Chrysler) in the event of accidental death;
3. freedom of worker choice in specifying *any* beneficiary. In the absence of a named beneficiary, the face amount of insurance was payable to the worker's estate;

---

[e]For example, group insurance benefits for the group studied exceeded the average group insurance coverage for working males in the United States. As this latter figure includes executive policies, the UAW coverage must exceed that for industrial workers. (*Life Insurance Fact Book,* 1967, p. 26.) (Data on total insurance coverage by industry are not presently available.) Similarly, the wages of auto workers are generally higher than those of many other industrial workers.

4. the right of the beneficiary to elect receipt of a single sum payment, or monthly, or yearly installments;

5. the terms of these installment options varied somewhat between companies. At one Big Three company, for example, monthly or annual installments could be taken for a maximum of 5 years. Interest was accrued at a guaranteed rate of 3% but could be greater as a result of the master policy provisions for allocation of distributable surpluses.

A significant departure from the reliance on lump sum survivor protection through group life insurance occurred in the 1964 auto negotiations. In addition to improving the basic group life insurance (by raising the amount of coverage at the upper and lower ends of the range to $6,000-$11,500, to reflect rising wages), new insurance and pension benefits were introduced (applicable to the survivors of the 1965 group of decedents) to provide, to a defined group of survivors, monthly income benefits for stipulated periods of time.[7]

The introduction of a new Automatic Survivor Pension for eligible widows in the 1964 auto agreements marked a major departure from the basic group life insurance approach to survivor protection. Under this new pension provision, a widow (of any age) of an active worker who died while eligible to retire (at age 60 or over with 10 year's of service, or at age 55 or over with a combination of his age plus years of service equalling the number 85), was automatically eligible for a Survivor Pension equal in amount to approximately 50% of the pension the worker would have been eligible to receive had he retired and elected a survivor pension option.

In the period covered in this report, the sample of widows interviewed were not eligible to receive such Automatic Survivor Pensions because entitlement is deferred until these survivors have exhausted certain new survivor income benefits also made available under the Insurance provisions of the 1964 collective bargaining agreements.

These new survivor income benefits, known as the Transition and Bridge Survivor Income benefits reflected, in part, a recognition of the fact that the problems of younger and older dependent survivors were believed to be particularly different. The Transition Survivor Income Benefit, provided specified classes of beneficiaries of deceased workers with the amount of $100 per month for up to 24 months, but no longer than the period that any eligible survivor remains alive. In the 1964 Agreement, such beneficiaries were limited to include first, only the widow or dependent widower. In the event that neither survived, any child or children under 21 years of age were provided for. In the event none of the former survived, the worker's dependent parents, if any, could be eligible. This benefit could only be taken as monthly income and could not be commuted in any part (that is, paid in a lump sum).

The second new benefit, the Bridge Survivor Income Benefit, begins in specified cases at the expiration of the Transition Benefit. Eligibility was limited under the 1964 agreement to widows and dependent widowers who were at least 50 years of age at the time of the worker's death. This benefit continues until the survivor reaches age 62. However, no benefit was paid if (1) the widow or widower remarries during this time; and (2) the widow is eligible for a mother's Social Security benefit during the period that she has a dependent child under her care. The amount of this benefit was also $100 per month and could not be commuted.

The term Bridge refers to the concept of bridging over the period from the time of the worker's death or, if there are children, from the time the youngest child ceases to be eligible for children's benefits under Social Security, to the age (62 years) where income support under the public program (OASDHI) resumes or first becomes available to the surviving spouse.

Unlike group life insurance, where beneficiaries are named at the discretion of the individual purchasing or covered by the contract, monthly payments of Transition and Bridge benefits may go only to the survivor classes noted above. Furthermore, these benefits were an addition to the lump sum life insurance benefits applicable to 1965 survivors and remain in effect (with increases in amount and a broadened group of covered beneficiaries), under the 1967 Agreements.

The 1967 Insurance programs retain the principle of spelling out an order of beneficiary classes, reflecting priorities of presumed need and supplement available benefits under public and private programs, in implicit recognition of their limitations. Such supplementation is particularly apt for widows with young children or those aged 50 years or over for many of whom suitable employment is not a realistic alternative.[f]

---

[f]The largest group of widows in the study were in their mid forties or older. Relatively few widows had had significant previous work experience. While many widows did find work, it is common knowledge that without previous experience and special skills, the job market for such widows is difficult, at best.

3

Characteristics of
Workers and Survivors

Demographic and other characteristics of the workers and survivors are presented in this chapter. The experiences and problems of the survivors are reported and analyzed in Chapters 4 - 6. To provide an appreciation of the subsamples of workers and their survivors, a brief profile is presented initially. Specific data regarding their characteristics then follow.

Key reference figures on the study sample with which data throughout Chapters 3 - 6 may be compared are provided in Table 3-1.

A Profile[a]

The modal (or most common) group among the 735 deceased workers who left dependent survivors (Dep.), and were interviewed on the Long Form (L.F.) questionnaire, died between the ages of 50 and 59; median age 56. The typical deceased worker was a native born American, Caucasian, and Protestant. Typically, he had not had any military service,[b] had not completed high school, was generally considered unskilled or semiskilled in that he had no special formal training as a journeyman or otherwise. In addition, he had been employed by his auto employer for 20 years or more. This typical deceased worker was married at the time of his death; of these, most had been married only once and for 20 or more years. Two percent had never been married, while 21% had been married two or three times. In more than half the cases, the deceased worker left dependents in addition to his wife. In 45% of the cases, however, the surviving family unit consisted of a wife only, with no other dependent survivors.

The 138 deceased workers in the total sample whose group insurance proceeds went to nondependent survivors (NonDep.) and who were interviewed on the Short Form (S.F.) questionnaire, showed characteristics generally similar to those who left dependents. However, the typical deceased worker in this subgroup had been widowed, divorced, or separated, and 38% had never been married.

---

[a]Except as noted, data refer to deceased workers and survivors for 1963 and 1965 combined. For a discussion of the means of sampling dependent and nondependent survivors, see Chapter 2 and Appendix B.

[b]Given the average age of the workers, this finding is somewhat surprising, unless it is explained by critical skills deferments in World War II. The workers involved would have been at the upper end of the draft age in World War II and generally too old for the Korean War.

The characteristics of these two samples of workers and their dependent or nondependent survivors will, to the extent feasible, be considered independently. This is essential if the nature and effectiveness of the group life insurance programs in the plans studied are to be fully understood and evaluated.

Table 3-1

Summary of Sample Key Numbers[a]

	1963	1965	1963 & 1965
Dependent Survivor Units (Long Form)	345	390	735
Nondependent Survivor Units (Short Form)	69	69	138
Dependent & Nondependent Survivor Units	414	459	873
Widows	325	367	692
Widows Remarried at Interview	26	4	30
Death by Illness	372	400	772
Death by Accident	37	64	101

Summary of Sample Key Percentages

	1963	1965	1963 & 1965
Dependent Survivor Units as % of All Survivor Units	83%	85%	84%
Widow Headed Dependent Survivor Units as % of all Dependent Survivor Units	94	94	94
Remarried Widows as % of all Widows	8	1	4
Accident.l Deaths as % of all Deaths	9	14	12

[a]In all tables where numbers are involved, the designation N= is used to present the applicable numbers on which percentages are based. Text information not based on tables is labeled "not shown" or "not shown in table."

Nature of Worker Illness and Death

In nine out of ten cases, the cause of the worker's death was illness rather than accident.[c] Among those dying of illness, the greatest single reported cause of death (over half) was heart disease.[d] Among those dying as a result of accident, nearly half (48%) occurred travelling to or from work (39%), or at work (9%).

Nearly one half of the deceased workers had been ill or injured and away from work nine or more full weeks in the 12 months preceding their death. Incidentally, 90% of those who were reported as having been off one week or more received the negotiated weekly Sickness and Accident Benefit as partial replacement of the income lost during the illness. The remainder were apparently ineligible for or had exhausted this benefit or there may have been reporting error by survivors not fully informed of their husband's income. Also, most of the deceased workers left no bills for hospital, doctor, or special medical services to be paid after death. For the majority of those who did, such bills averaged less than $100.[e]

For those workers whose group insurance proceeds went to nondependent survivors the picture, though less complete, is much the same. However, unlike those who left dependent survivors, most of the accidental deaths were unrelated to work. While no explicit explanation can be offered for this difference, it may be attributable to the different ages and activities of those workers without dependents. Among workers without dependent survivors, an even larger percentage of workers left no unpaid health care bills or only very small charges. This was at least partially attributable to the higher percentage of accidental deaths among those not leaving dependent survivors.

The Group Insurance Beneficiaries

The typical dependent recipient of the group insurance proceeds was a widow with dependent children. The modal age group of the widows at the time of

---

[c]Though not standardized for age, race or sex, it is notable that nationally, in 1965, the death rate for the United States population by accidents, was approximately 6% of the rate for all causes. *Statistical Abstract of the United States, 1967*, Table 69. Of more direct comparison is a study reported in *Transactions, Society of Actuaries, 1965 Report Number*. This study, including all accidental deaths covered by major group insurers (1955-1964) reveals that accidental death claims represented 9.5% of all death claims in the auto industry.(p. 151). Thus, the workers studied were typical auto workers in this respect. For all workers covered, the ratio was 9.1%.(p. 159).

[d]This is consistent with national data which also indicate that heart disease is the greatest single cause of death for the total population, *Statistical Abstract of the United States, 1967*.

[e]This finding is consistent with the relatively high quality and comprehensiveness of the UAW negotiated health insurance benefits covering these workers. The death related expenses reported by survivors are lower than would be expected of those with less comprehensive health protection.

interview was between 50 and 59. The median age at this time was 53 years, compared to a median age for deceased workers of 56 years. Thus, adjusting for the time since the worker's death, the typical widow was generally *more* than four years younger than her deceased husband.

In general, like her husband, the widow was a native born white American Protestant. Typically, she had not completed high school (though on average, she was somewhat better educated than her husband) and had not taken additional special courses or vocational education. In most cases, the widow was not working at the time of her husband's death. However, most of the widows reported some outside work experience, either at the time of their husband's death or at some time prior to his death.[f]

At the time of the interview, (28 to 40 months after the worker's death) a relatively large percentage (about half) of the 1963 widow survivors were working either full or part time. This is considerably greater than the U.S. percentage of widows working in 1966 (36%). The relative difference in the prefatality and postfatality working records of the widows studied is also of interest. It offers indirect evidence of the economic adjustment problems of such widows.

A smaller percentage of the 1965 widow survivors were working at the time of interview (4 to 16 months after the worker's death). In almost half the cases involving dependent survivors, some Social Security Benefits were being received. In addition, nearly nine out of ten of the 1965 dependent survivors were receiving the $100/month UAW negotiated Transition Survivor Income Benefit that was introduced as a result of the 1964 negotiations.[g]

Of the nondependent recipients of the deceased worker's group life insurance, most were siblings, children, or parents (including in-laws). Only 8% of the nondependent recipients (1% of all those sampled) were not related at all to the deceased worker. Most of the nondependent recipients reported having seen the deceased worker daily during the last year of his life. A substantial additional group reported seeing the deceased more than once a week or once a month. Thus, in the large majority of cases involving nondependent beneficiaries, a close prefatality relationship to the deceased was reported.

---

[f]Though 30% of the widows studied reported themselves as working at the time of their husband's death, 35% of all United States wives were estimated as working in 1965. Given the age distribution of the widows studied (high average age) the difference is even greater than indicated. Though it is known that the increased number of working wives has been heavily influenced by the employment of more educated women, the above difference was not expected by the authors. *Statistical Abstract of the United States,* 1967, Table 324.

[g]Though all workers were eligible for this benefit, some of the deceased may not have been at work on the effective date of the benefit, and other survivors may have mistakenly reported the absence of the benefit.

**Demographic Social and Economic
Characteristics of Deceased Workers**

Age

The sample of deceased workers covered in the study had a median age of 56, as shown in Table 3-2.

In general, the age distribution in the 1963 and 1965 subsamples is quite similar, indicating that age of the worker is not a major source of variation in survivor adjustment patterns for the two years. Table 3-2 presents the age distribution of the sample by class of beneficiary. Comparison with other industrial groups or other groups of auto workers is not possible since comparable data for such populations are not presently available.

Moreover, the impact of varying compulsory retirement provisions would make analysis of such data difficult. Though not shown in the table, workers leaving nondependent survivors represented only 16% of the total sample, these workers included 68% of those in the total sample under age 25 and 56% of all those over 65.

Marital Status

More than nine out of ten of those leaving dependent survivors were reported as married at the time of their death.

As a matter of interest, 6% of those workers who left the proceeds of their group life insurance to nondependent survivors were reported as having been married at the time of their death, but this may involve interview errors.

Age and Family Composition

The family composition in the two survey years was similar, as indicated in Table 3-4.

Again, this variable cannot be cited in explaining adjustment differences between the subsamples of survivors. Almost half of the deceased workers (45%) resided in family units with their wives and no other dependents. Approximately one out of six of the widow-headed surviving families had more than two dependents in addition to the widow.

On the question of possible work opportunities for widows with children, it is notable that very few, less than 10% of the nonremarried widow-headed surviving units, reported dependents under 13 years of age.

Excluding the widow, 87% of the dependent survivors were under the age of 19.

Some 6% of dependent survivors were children, parents, or otherwise dependent on the deceased worker in families in which no widow was reported as surviving the deceased worker.

Table 3-2

**Age of Workers (% Distribution)
1963 & 1965**

	Nondep.[a]	Dep.	Dep. & Nondep.
N =	138	735	873
%N =	16%	84%	100%
Age			
< 25	11%	1%	2%
25-34	3	4	3
35-44	10	10	10
45-54	22	31	30
55-64	35	51	49
65+	17	3	5
No Answer	1	*	1
	100%**	100%	100%
Median[b]	56	56	56
Mean	51	53	53

[a]Nondep. (Nondependent) indicates those workers not leaving dependent beneficiaries (interviewed on Short Form).

Dep. (Dependent) indicates those workers leaving dependent beneficiaries (interviewed on Long Form).

[b]Calculation of Median based on group formula found in John E. Freund, *Modern Elementary Statistics,* Second Edition, p. 59.

*Less than 0.6% (Note: *used in all subsequent tables)

**Tables may not always add to 100% due to rounding; hereafter referred to as "rounding error." (Note: ** used in all subsequent tables)

Table 3-3

Marital Status of Workers (% Distribution)
1963 & 1965

	Nondep.	Dep.	Dep. & Nondep.
N =	138	735	873
%N =	16%	84%	100%
Marital Status			
Married	6%	94%	80%
Widowed	18	1	4
Divorced	29	2	6
Separated	9	1	2
Never Married	38	2	7
No Answer	1	*	*
	100%**	100%	100%**

Country of Origin and Citizenship

Though approximately 15% of the total sample (130) were born outside the United States,[h] only five of the workers (less than 1%) were not citizens at the time of their death. All of the foreign born Americans had lived in the United States for 10 or more years; over 90% lived here for 30 years or more.

Table 3-7 summarizes the worker's country of birth. Well over half of the workers' fathers had also been born in the United States (not shown in table). A somewhat higher than expected percentage of the Canadian born workers left no dependent survivors. This cannot be explained by the data available.

Religion

In the samples for both years, over half the workers were Protestant. Among the Baptists, 67% of the blacks (not shown in table) and a large number of Southern whites are represented, reflecting their migration to Detroit during World War II

---

[h]Approximately 7% of the urban U.S. population in 1960 were foreign born. The percentage of foreign born in Michigan in 1960 was somewhat higher (9%). No data are currently available regarding the percentage of foreign born population in Detroit, but it apparently exceeds 9%. *Statistical Abstract of the United States,* 1967, Tables 14, 25 and 29.

Table 3-4

**Size of Families (Dependent Beneficiaries)
1963 & 1965**

Family Composition	Families	
(Number of dependents in family)	*Number*	*Percent*
1963		
Worker and:		
Wife only	162	48%
Wife and one	67	20
Wife and two	45	13
Wife and three	25	7
Wife and four (or more)	26	8
Miscellaneous dependents [a]	15	4
	340	100%
1965		
Worker and:		
Wife only	172	44%
Wife and one	79	20
Wife and two	54	14
Wife and three	27	7
Wife and four (or more)	35	9
Miscellaneous dependents	28	7
	395	100%**
1963 & 1965		
Worker and:		
Wife only	334	45
Wife and one	146	20
Wife and two	99	13
Wife and three	52	7
Wife and four (or more)	61	8
Miscellaneous dependents	43	6
	735	100%**

[a]Includes worker's parents or families where wife predeceased worker.

Table 3-5

Age of Youngest Dependent Child[a]
(% Distribution)

	1963	*1965*
N =	325	367
None	65%	56%
< 5 years	1	3
5-12 years	6	9
13-17 years	18	19
18-20 years	11	12
	100**	100**

[a]Children under 21; widow-headed dependent survivor units.

Table 3-6

Age of Dependent Survivors[a]
(% Distribution)

	1963		1965	
Age	*%*	*Cumulative %*	*%*	*Cumulative %*
N =	382		483	
< 10 years	31%	31%	31%	31%
10-19 years	57	88	55	86
20-29 years	7	95	7	93
30-39 years	1	96	1	94
40 and over	4	100	5	99**

[a]Excludes widows.

Table 3-7

Worker's Country of Origin (% Distribution)
1963 & 1965

	Nondep.	Dep.	Dep. & Nondep.
N =	138	735	873
%N =	16%	84%	100%
Country			
U.S.A.	86%	85%	85%
Canada	4	2	3
Other	9	13	12
	100%**	100%**	100%**

Table 3-8

Worker's Religious Preference
(% Distribution) 1963 & 1965

	Nondep.	Dep.	Dep. & Nondep.
N =	138	735	873
%N =	16%	84%	100%
Religion			
Protestant	55%	58%	58%
Catholic	39	36	37
Other	3	2	2
None	3	3	3
No Answer	*	*	*
	100%	100%	100%

Table 3-9

Worker's Protestant Denomination
(% Distribution) 1963 & 1965

	Nondep.	*Dep.*	*Dep. & Nondep.*
N =	76%	429	505
%N =	15%	85%	100%
Protestant Denomination			
Baptist	41%	40%	40%
Methodist	20	18	19
Lutheran	10	16	15
Episc.-Presb.-Cong.	17	10	11
Other	9	15	14
No Answer	3	*	1
	100%	100%**	100%

and later. It is difficult to predict, *a priori,* the precise nature of the impact of this variable, particularly as other variables to be considered, for example, such factors as income, race, and education, often intervene and complicate or dominate the impact.

Race

Data on racial characteristics were obtained by interviewer observation of the respondent, in most cases the beneficiary. While race is a potentially significant variable in the explanation of cultural attitudes toward death and adjustment, intervening variables, (such as income, education, time resident in Detroit, and religion) again make analysis based on race quite difficult.

Caucasians represented 79% of all the deceased workers in the study year 1963, and 21% were black, as indicated in Table 3-10 below.

In 1965, 23% were black.[i] The statistical significance of the increased percentage of blacks among the deceased in 1965 was not tested.

---

[i]This proportion is almost identical to the ratio of whites to nonwhites living in Michigan Central Cities during 1960 where the percentages were 77% white and 23% nonwhite. The corresponding percentages for Detroit were 71% white and 29% nonwhite. No comparable figures are available for 1963 or 1965. The sources of these data are: U.S. Bureau of Census, U.S. Census of Population: 1960 *General Population Characteristics, Michigan.* Final Report PC (1)-24B, Table 14 and *The Statistical Abstract of the United States,* 1967, Table 17.

Table 3-10

Age and Race of Deceased Workers
(% Distribution)

Age	1963			1965		
	Total[a]	Caucasian	Black	Total[a]	Caucasian	Black
N =	409	322	86	464	354	106
%N =	100%	79%	21%	100%	76%	23%
25	1%	1%	*%	4%	4%	6%
25-34	3	3	1	4	3	6
35-44	9	7	19	11	10	16
45-54	32	33	27	28	27	32
55-64	50	50	48	51	54	40
65 +	5	6	3	2	2	1
No Answer	1	*	2	*	*	*
	100%**	100%	100%	100%**	100%**	100**
Median	56	56	56	56	56	52
Mean	54	54	53	52	53	50

[a]Includes Orientals and no answer.

For the group as a whole, 22 percent were black.

Table 3-11 presents data on the deceased worker's race by dependent status of his beneficiaries. The apparent difference in racial composition of these subgroups is largely accounted for by the percentage of no answer and other reported for the workers leaving no dependent survivors.

The median age at death was the same for both Caucasians and blacks in the 1963 group, but in 1965 the median age of black workers at death (52 years) was about four years less than that of whites. The source of this difference was not specifically investigated and it may be attributable to chance variations. Among the United States population as a whole, nonwhites typically die younger than whites.

Table 3-11

Worker's Race (% Distribution)
1963 & 1965

	Nondep.	*Dep.*	*Dep. & Nondep.*
N =	138	735	873
%N =	16%	84%	100%
Race			
Caucasian	74%	78%	77%
Black	23	22	22
Other	1	*	*
No Answer	2	*	*
	100%	100%	100%**

Education

With respect to educational level, the distributions of deceased workers for the two sample years and for workers leaving dependent and nondependent survivors are quite comparable, as indicated in Table 3-12.

Twenty-one percent of the deceased workers received a high school education or better. Near half of those studied attained an eight grade education or less. This attainment must be judged against the average age of the workers.

As shown in Table 3-26, the worker's wives were somewhat better educated. Excluding the 8% of the survivors who did not know the educational attainment of the deceased worker, the worker-wife educational differences are more pronounced. For example, on this basis, 49% of the workers were reported as having had an eighth grade education or less. This compared with 37% of the widows with similar educational attainment.

Work Life

For the total sample of deceased workers, the average number of years of service (with last employer) was 23 years, generally acknowledged as long service in the auto and other industries.

Table 3-12

**Worker's Education (% Distribution)
1963 & 1965**

	Nondep.	*Dep.*	*Nondep. & Dep.*
N =	138	735	873
%N =	16%	84%	100%
School Completed			
Eighth grade or less	43%	45%	45%
Some high school	25	27	27
Completed high school	17	16	16
Some college[a]	4	*	5
Don't know	11	7	8
	100%	100%**	100%**

[a]Four workers (1965) had completed college.

This is consistent with the age of the workers involved, in that relatively few persons over 40 years of age are entering industrial employment. The sample groups cannot be directly compared with explicit industry or company records since the age-service distribution of comparable populations in the periods covered is unknown. Median and mean years of service for workers leaving nondependent survivors are somewhat less than that for the remaining workers. This reflects the higher portion of accidental deaths (particularly those not work-related) among the former category of workers.

Approximately half of the workers studied (45%) were classed as unskilled in the categorization developed for this study. The remainder of the workers divided almost equally between semiskilled (29%) and skilled (26%). Relatively few of the workers not leaving dependent survivors were in the highest skill category.

The skill distribution of Big Three auto workers in the Detroit area is not known for the periods in which deaths occurred.

Skill category (as used in this study) is recognized to be an imperfect measure since it was based on the worker's hourly wage groupings (used for insurance purposes). In automobile plants, as elsewhere, relatively higher wages compensate the skilled as well as those performing what many consider to be disagreeable tasks, for example, any work under extreme temperature or noise conditions. In addition, worker skill is correlated with age and length of service.

Table 3-13

Worker's Length of Service
(% Distribution) 1963 & 1965

	Nondep.	*Dep.*	*Dep. & Nondep.*
N =	138	735	873
%N =	16%	84%	100%
Years of Service			
0- 9	17%	12%	13
10-19	33	30	30
20-29	26	26	26
30-39	19	27	26
40-49	4	4	4
50-59	*	*	*
No Answer	1	1	1
	100%	100%	100%
Median	20	23	23
Mean	21	23	23

Still, the validity of the skill classification used is indicated by the rough conformity of the distribution of those completing high school (Table 3-12) with those considered to be highly skilled (Category III), and the unskilled group (I) with those with less than an eighth grade education.

Table 3-15 relating worker skill and special training, adds further support to the use of the skill variable as a supplement to other measures of income.

In considering the skill variable, the following data (not shown in the tables) are notable:

a. While 16% of the sample left no dependent beneficiaries, only 8% of category III (highly skilled) workers left no dependent beneficiaries.
b. The median age at death of category III workers was 56 years (1963) and 57 years (1965). This was one and two years older than the age at death for category I and II workers in 1963. In 1965, the respective difference was two and three years.

40

Table 3-14

Worker's Skill Category
(% Distribution) 1963 & 1965

	Nondep.	Dep.	Dep. & Nondep.	Potential Income[a] 1963	1965
N =	138	735	873		
%N =	16%	84%	100%		
Skill Category					
I	57%	42%	45%	Under $6500	Under $7000
II	30	29	29	$6500-7000	$7000-$7500
III	12	28	26	Over $7000	Over $7500
	100%**	100%**	100%		

[a]The potential annual income of the workers in the above skill categories (assuming full time employment). The worker's negotiated group insurance is set to equal approx approximately 110% of expected annual wage income. (See also note c, Appendix A.)

Table 3-15

Worker Skill and Training (% Distribution)
1963 & 1965

	% With Specialized Training		
Skill Category	Nondep.	Dep.	Dep. & Nondep.
I	20%	21%	21%
II	29	28	28
III	59	71	70

Work and Family Income

In absolute terms, total prefatality family income was derived by combining an estimate of the worker's wage income plus the reported earnings of other family members. Median hourly wage rate was derived from insurance company records of insurance coverage. It was assumed that 2080 hours per year were worked. This is an overestimate for some workers, particularly those who were ill. However, it understates the hours worked of those with significant overtime. The income derived by multiplying the hourly rate and estimate of hours worked is, in effect, an estimate of potential earnings and as such is indicative of the family's potential standard of living.

Table 3-16 summarizes the distribution of prefatality worker and family income. The median worker wage income of those leaving dependent survivors was $5730 (1963) and $6220 (1965). The corresponding median for those not leaving dependent survivors (not shown) was $5710 (1963) and $5920 (1965). Median family income was $6900 (1963) and $7410 (1965). Thus, median dependents' earnings were $1170 (1963) and $1190 (1965).

The DCWFB described in Chapter 2 could not be applied to this prefatality income (as an indicator of adequacy) since no set of equivalent incomes (for varying family sizes and including applicable taxes) exists. Attempts to indicate adequacy by comparing postfatality income and prefatality income fail because of changes in family size, tax requirements, and so on. Still, on the basis of figures cited and a selective adjustment of DCWFB data to reflect taxes, it appears that the standard included in the DCWFB updated to the year of death, is one which had been met by nearly all auto worker families while the chief wage earner was living.

While as mentioned above, no explicit measure of the adequacy of prefatality income is feasible, some partial guide to its adequacy is provided by certain financial data. For example, almost 80% of the workers owned their own home at the time of death. This is consistent with the percentage of home ownership in Detroit. Almost half of the homeowners in the sample held clear title (without a mortgage); the remainder owed from $5000-$7000 on homes having a median market value of $13,000. (68 respondents, however, were unwilling or unable to estimate the value of their home.)ʲ

Nature of Worker's Illness and Death

For nearly 90% of the total sample, illness rather than accident was the cause of death.

Of those not leaving dependent survivors, however, illness accounted for less

---

ʲAs a further approximate indicator of the modesty of the DCWFB standard, the 1959 DCWFB (updated to 1966) assumes for example that a modest but adequate standard for a family of 4 includes a 5 room rented home or apartment costing $87 per month, including utilities. "The Interim City Worker's Family Budget," Helen H. Lamale and Margaret S. Stotz, *Monthly Labor Review,* August 1960, p. 789. A further discussion of this standard is included in Chapter 2 and Appendix A. For the small percentage of renters in the study, the average reported rental (exclusive of utilities) was $70 per month.

Table 3-16

Prefatality Income[a]
(% Distribution)

Annual Income	Worker's Income		Family Income	
	1963	1965	1963	1965
N =[a]	340	395	322	354
$4000-$4999	2%	–	1%	–
5000- 5999	66	48%	34	19%
6000- 6999	10	24	16	23
7000- 7999	19	21	19	19
8000- 8999	2	4	11	12
9000- 9999	1	3	6	9
10000-10999	–	–	5	6
11000-11999	–	–	5	6
12000 +	–	–	3	6
	100%	100%	100%	100%
Median	$5730	$6220	$6900	$7410

[a]Excludes those for whom family income
could not be calculated.

than 80% of the deaths. Of all those dying of illness, approximately 50% were
reported as having died of heart disease, (44% of all deaths in the study). Among
those dying as a result of an accident, nearly half died at work or travelling to or
from work (as already indicated).

Nearly two-thirds of the deceased workers had been sick and away from work
for more than a week during the twelve months preceding their death.

Of this group (not shown in the table), 60% had been off sick for nine or
more weeks. While sick, most of the deceased workers (90%) drew Accident and
Sickness benefits as partial replacement of lost wage income.

Table 3-20 summarizes age and type of death. In this case, age also serves as a
proxy for length of service, since it is known that these are highly correlated. As
indicated in this table and earlier, illness caused roughly ten times as many
deaths as accidents. As expected, the percentage of accident caused deaths as a
percent of all deaths, declines with age (not shown). Whereas only 12% of the

Table 3-17

Cause of Death (% Distribution)
1963 & 1965

	Nondep.	*Dep.*	*Dep. & Nondep.*
N =	138	735	873
%N =	16%	84%	100%
Cause of Death			
Illness	78%	90%	88%
Accident[a]	22	10	11
	100%	100%	100%**

aIncludes murder, suicide, or ambiguous report

Table 3-18

Illness as Cause of Worker's Death
(%Distribution) 1963 & 1965

	Nondep.	*Dep.*	*Dep. & Nondep.*
N =	108	664	772
%N =	14%	86%	100%
Illness			
Heart Disease	45%	51%	50%
Cancer	23	23	23
Stroke	7	5	5
Respiratory	4	3	2
Diabetes	1	1	1
Other	18	18	18
Don't know	2	*	*
	100%	100%**	100%

Table 3-19

Weeks Off Sick[a] (% Distribution) 1963 & 1965

N =	735
None	38%
4 weeks or less	13
5-12 weeks	20
13-28 weeks	18
29-44 weeks	5
45-52 weeks	5
No Answer	1
	100%

[a]Workers leaving dependent survivors only;
information not available for other workers.
Covers 12-month period preceding death.

workers succumbed to illness before age 45, the majority of accidental deaths occurred before that age.

A Profile of Beneficiaries[k]

Age

As expected, the widows were somewhat younger than the deceased workers. At the time of interview, which was up to 40 months after their husband's death, their median age was 53 compared to median husband's age at death of 56 (Table 3-2). The interview of 1963 widows occurred 28 to 40 months after the worker's death, placing their median age at the time of death at approximately 51. For 1965 widows, their husband's death occurred 4 to 16 months earlier, placing their median age at approximately 52. The median difference in ages is thus 4-5 years for the two years combined.

The actual distribution of worker-wife age differences reveals that 57% of all workers were within a year of their wife's age or older at the time of the worker's death. While 10% of the deceased workers were 11 or more years older

[k]Except where specified, widows are described. The number of family units headed by a nonwidow dependent beneficiary is too small to consider meaningfully. The demographic characteristics of nondependent beneficiaries are not covered in detail as this was beyond the scope of the study.

Table 3-20

Age and Cause of Death
(% Distribution) 1963 & 1965

	Accident	Illness
N =	80	793
%N =	9%	91%
Age		
< 25	18%	1%
25-34	21	1
35-44	18	10
45-54	28	31
55-64	16	52
65 +	*	4
No Answer	*	1
	100%	100%
Median	41	56
Mean	40	54

than their wives; only 1% of the wives exceeded their husband's age by this amount.

Country of Origin

Like their deceased husbands, the vast majority (88%) of widows had been born in the United States. Of the remainder, one-third had been born in Canada.

Of all foreign born widows, 80% had become citizens by the time of the interview (not shown). Two percent of the foreign born widows had lived in the United States for less than nine years, but, 80% had lived here for 30 years or more. Over 60% of the widows' fathers had been born in the United States. Thus, both the widows and their deceased husbands were predominantly American born or had become citizens. (The negotiated benefits in no way require citizenship.)

Table 3-21

Age of Widow (% Distribution)
(At Interview)

Age	1963	1965	1963 & 1965
N=	325	367	692
< 20	*	*	*
20-29	1%	4%	3%
30-39	6	8	7
40-49	23	27	25
50-59	47	44	46
60-69	21	16	18
70 +	2	1	1
No Answer	*	*	*
	100%	100%	100%
Median	54	53	53
Mean	52	52	52

Table 3-22

Worker-Wife Age Difference[a]
(% Distribution)

	N	Years Wife Older			Worker-Wife Same Age[b]	Years Worker Older			
		11-18	5-10	2-4		2-5	6-10	11-15	16-28
1963	323	1%	3%	5%	17%	38%	26%	8%	2%
1965	367	1	3	6	21	38	22	7	2
1963 + 1965	690	1	3	6	19	38	24	8	2

[a]Obtained by adjusting widows age at interview by average time lapsed since worker's death.

[b]As date of worker's death was not cited, same age includes year younger or older.

Table 3-23

**Country of Origin—Widows
(% Distribution) 1963 & 1965**

Country of Birth

N =	692
U.S.A.	88
Canada	4
Other	8
No Answer	*
	100%

Table 3-24

**Widow's Religion (% Distribution)
1963 & 1965**

N =	692
Protestant	60%
Catholic	37
Other	2
None	1
No Answer	*
	100%

Religion

Widows expressed essentially identical religious preference to that reported for their deceased husband. While it is not known if the couples were of the same religious denomination at marriage or if one or both had converted, it had been expected that reported religious differences would be minimal.

Table 3-24 reports the widows' religious denomination. For Protestants, the denomination is reported in Table 3-25.

Table 3-25

**Widow's Protestant Denomination
(% Distribution) 1963 & 1965**

N =	418
Baptist	42%
Methodist	20
Lutheran	16
Episc.-Presb.-Cong.	10
Other	13
	100%**

Table 3-26

**Educational Background of Widow
(% Distribution) 1963 & 1965**

Last Grade Completed

N =	692
Eighth grade or less	37%
Some high school	32
High school	26
Some college[a]	4
No Answer	*
	100%**

[a]Includes 5 widows who completed college.

Table 3-27

**Widows Working at Time
of Husband's Death
(% Distribution) 1963 & 1965**

	% of those working	% of group
N =		692
Yes, full time	73%	22%
(N = 209)		
Yes, part time	27	8
No (N = 483)		70
		100%

Table 3-28

**Relation of Nondependent Beneficiary[a]
to Deceased Worker (% Distribution)**

	1963	1965	1963 & 1965
N =	69	69	138
Former wife	3%	1%	2%
Child	26	26	26
Parent	14	30	22
Sibling	34	32	33
Other relative	12	4	8
Other non-relative	10	6	8
	100%**	100%**	100%**

[a]Not all beneficiaries were interviewed.
Another respondent (not the beneficiary) answered for the beneficiary in
15% of these interviews.

Education

The educational background of the widow for both years is comparable to (if not somewhat stronger than) that of her deceased husband. As indicated in Table 3-26, 30% reported completion of high school or beyond (as compared with only 21% of the workers). In addition, 26% of the widows reported having taken special courses or vocational training (not shown in the table). For more than half of the widows with some special training, the training was in office skills. Almost 15% of the special training was for nursing or teaching.

Viewed against the widow's typical age (median 53 at interview) the above education and training do not suggest a high likelihood of securing employment in her field of training or otherwise.

Work Life

Nearly a third (30%) of the widows were working full or part time at the time of their husband's death. Their work included domestic service (15% of those working), labor, and factory work (19%), retail sales (27%), and clerical work (23%). Of those not working at the time of their husband's death or at the time of interview, two-thirds had work experience at some time prior to the worker's death. Work status relates, as expected, to age and family status.

Nondependent Beneficiaries

In almost all cases (91%) the nondependent beneficiary was a relative of the deceased worker by blood or marriage. Nearly half (44%) of these beneficiaries had been living in the worker's household at the time of his death (not shown). Over half (55%) of all the nondependent respondents saw the deceased worker daily during the last year of his life (not shown). Thus, even in the case of nondependent beneficiaries a close personal relationship generally existed between the deceased worker and his beneficiary.

In this chapter, a description of the basic characteristics of the deceased workers, their illness, and their survivors has been presented. Though survivor benefit programs are not directly keyed to most of the variables discussed, they are of interest and importance in evaluating existing programs and in planning future survivor benefit programs.

4

Economic Impact of the Breadwinner's Death

In the previous chapter, a profile of deceased workers and their insurance beneficiaries was presented. In this chapter, the immediate and ongoing economic impact of the breadwinner's death on the largest group of survivors—those surviving units headed by widows—is examined. Specific consideration of dependent survivor units headed by other than widows is omitted because of their small number (15 - 1963 and 28 - 1964; 4% and 7% of dependent survivor cases).

Immediate Financial Adjustments

Predeath work and family income was summarized in Chapter 3. In general, it was assumed to provide at least a modest but adequate standard of living. The financial adjustments necessitated by the death of the primary wage earner derive from the worker's liabilities at death, either existing or created directly and indirectly by his death, and the resources available to meet such liabilities. These adjustments may lead the widow or other survivors to seek employment or make other modifications in their modes of living. In the long run, if the widow remarries or becomes wholly or partially self-supporting, or dependent children become similarly independent, additional adjustments are possible.

Immediate adjustments are assumed to involve those death-related expenses that are directly related to the worker's death and are generally considered current obligations following it. The worker's funeral is the most obvious example of an immediate adjustment item. Other items include current personal debts and estate fees. It is assumed that one function of insurance is to provide funds to help meet such costs. Therefore, immediate adjustment adequacy was inferred by comparing death-related expenses with resources created (for example, life insurance proceeds) by the death.

The Detroit City Worker's Family Budget (described in Chapter 2 and Appendix B) was the major indicator of ongoing economic adequacy used to evaluate generally postdeath financial adjustments of widow-headed families. Family income was compared to the modest but adequate income standard suggested by updating the 1959 CWFB to reflect changing costs in the Detroit area. Such a standard permits avoidance of direct consideration of dollar incomes, (the value and utility of which change over time and vary by demographic status) and substitutes a composite measure which incorporates income, family size, and age of family head and dependents. As indicated in Chapter 2, though not without its own limitations (for example, adequate involves value judgements, and so on) the DCWFB standard provides a basic measure of adequacy of income as defined.

Conceptually then, in a financial sense, the death of the worker destroyed his income potential and related benefits, for example, negotiated company paid health insurance, as well as his productivity in the home (as gardner, repairman), and created death-related expenses. Simultaneously, group insurance proceeds were created, along with (in many cases) lump sum burial and monthly Social Security benefits, private life insurance benefits, other public lump sum and monthly benefits (for example, Veterans Insurance) and monthly survivor income benefits (Transition and Bridge for most 1965 survivors). In addition, (though the extent is not known precisely for the group studied), for many survivors, previously mortgaged assets may now be held free and clear as a result of mortgage or credit insurance covering the purchase of these assets.

Given the above financial net change, the *immediate* financial adjustment of the surviving family is defined (for purposes of this chapter) as a comparison of the lump sum resources created by the death and the death-related expenses. Adequate *ongoing* adjustment (for purposes of this study) is viewed as meeting daily living requirements as indicated by comparing family income and the specified budget standard (DCWFB). Such adjustment is a function of such variables as initial financial status, net assets, family size, and age of dependents.

Financial Proceeds from the Death of the Worker

The single benefit covering all workers in the study was their lump sum group life insurance, median amounts—$6660 (1963) and $7050 (1965).[a] In addition, for the two years studied, 60% of the survivors reported receiving individual life (56%) or mortgage retirement (4%) insurance benefits. In fact, four out of five survivors reported some additional insurance benefits or other death benefit besides the negotiated survivor protection and Social Security benefits, if any.[b]

Total lump sum resources created by the death of the worker derived from the above insurance coverages. The median amounts of such resources were $7330 (1963) and $8270 (1965). Thus, in median terms, the workers studied had modest coverage in addition to the group insurance—$670 (1963) and $1220 (1965). The above figures may be somewhat misleading in that they are

---

[a]This is considered in detail in Chapter 5, when the survivors' uses of the group insurance proceeds are also examined. Median amount cited omits survivors electing to receive the lump sum benefit in installments.

[b]A 1960 survey by the Life Insurance Agency Management Association reported in "Life Insurance in Focus," reveals (Chapter V) that 77% of those heads of husband-wife families (age 45-64; income $5000-$8999) who were covered by group life insurance also carried individual insurance. This compares with 80% of the same group without group coverage who carried individual insurance. Thus, though no data for a group identical to the group presently studied are available, the above data indicate that the workers studied had total insurance protection at least roughly comparable to others in the same income and age range also covered by group insurance. (The above data were made available by the Institute of Life Insurance.)

Table 4-1

Additional Death Benefits[a]
(% Distribution)

	1963 % of Group Covered[b]	1965 % of Group Covered[b]	1963 & 1965 % of Group Covered[b]
N =	340	395	735
Workmen's Compensation & Public Liability	4%	2%	3%
Veterans Insurance	8	9	9
Private Life Insurance	58	54	56
Mortgage Retirement Insurance	5	4	4
Credit Union & Fraternal Life Insurance	8	25	17
Credit Insurance	21	34	28
Other	10	13	12
Total Additional Benefits[b]	385	556	941
Number with Additional Benefits	260	327	587
Number without Additional Benefits	80	68	148
% Without Additional Benefits	24%	17%	20%

[a]Nonwork group and nongovernment; excludes nondependent survivors. 97% of the 1963 survivors and 96% of the 1965 survivors had applied for the lump sum burial benefit provided under the Social Security Act. In only 4 cases (both years) was it reported that the undertaker had applied for this benefit directly.

[b]As some workers had more than one coverage total does not add to 100%.

for all the workers studied. As those with no dependent survivors are likely to have smaller amounts of nongroup insurance, the above figures understate the amount of private insurance actually carried by workers with dependent survivors.

For workers (leaving dependent survivors) having coverage in addition to their group insurance, median amounts of private insurance coverage (excluding credit insurance) of $1110 (1963) and $1370 (1965) were reported.

No attempt was made to estimate the commuted value of non-lump sum insurance proceeds as few survivors received such proceeds. Moreover, the survivor's knowledge of the terms of the monthly income involved were generally insufficient to permit estimation of a commuted value.

Table 4-2

Private Lump Sum Insurance[a]
(% Distribution)

Amount	1963	1965
N =	263	328
< $ 500	17%	12%
$ 500 - 999	26	19
1000 - 1499	32	35
1500 - 1999	6	7
2000 - 2999	11	7
3000 - 4999	3	14
5000 - 6999	3	2
7000 +	2	4
	100%	100%
Median	$1110	$1370

[a]Workers leaving dependent survivors; lump sum amounts excluding specific burial allowances reported as private life insurance, fraternal insurance or travel accident insurance.

Table 4-3

Debts Payable at Worker's Death

Debts	1963	1965
N =	101	69
< $ 500	38%	23%
$ 500 - $ 900	28	26
1000 - 1499	18	12
1500 - 1999	10	12
2000 - 2499	2	9
2500 +	5	19
	100%**	100%**
Median Debt	$732	$1263
% reporting debt	30%	17%

[a]Dependent survivors; excludes mortgages and other debts on tangible assets.
**Rounding error.

In general, in addition to higher average group insurance, 1965 workers were better protected than their 1963 counterparts in terms of percent covered by additional insurance and in size of policy. Major coverage differences were in Credit Union and Fraternal Life Insurance and Credit Insurance. In percentage terms, the 1965 group had fewer basic life insurance policies in force than the 1963 group. In absolute and percentage terms, the growth of credit insurance is reflected by the growth of this form of coverage among the group studied. This growth is even more significant when compared to the use of credit which actually declined among the 1965 workers.

While no estimate was made of the value of the assets that accrued to survivors as a result of credit life insurance policies paying off the balance due on a debt, the interview schedule does permit calculation of the total lump sum cash resources that were generated by the worker's death.

Table 4-4 summarizes the cash resources created by the death. Monthly Social Security and other regular income benefits are omitted. As indicated earlier, the total lump sum resources created as a result of the worker's death were somewhat higher in the 1965 group.

Table 4-4

Death Created Lump Sum Resources[a]
(% Distribution)

$ Resources		1963 Dep.	Nondep.	All	1965 Dep.	Nondep.	All
N =		329	69	398	384	69	453
<	1000[b]	3%	7%	*	3%	4%	1%
$ 1000 -	4999	3	7	8%	3	4	3
5000 -	5999	2	12	8	-	1	3
6000 -	6999	30	61	36	15	59	22
7000 -	7999	20	14	19	20	22	20
8000 -	8999	17	4	15	20	7	18
9000 -	9999	10	1	8	14	4	13
10000 -	19999	16	-	13	26	1	23
20000 -		1	-	1	1	-	1
		100%**	100%**	100%	100%**	100%**	100%**
Median		$7710	$6520	$7330	$8610	$6760	$8270

[a]Total of all insurance (excluding installment settlements) received after worker's death. All beneficiaries excluding those (22) with monthly benefits or for whom data are incomplete.

[b]Includes two reporting no group insurance benefits; benefits either delayed in processing or omitted as a result of reporting error.

*Less than 0.6%

**May not add due to rounding

In addition to the lump sum benefits generated as a result of the worker's death, claims to monthly income also accrued to survivors as a direct result of the death. For more than half of the dependent survivors, such income (including Social Security, if any, but excluding the Transition Benefit which went to nine out of ten 1965 dependent survivors) is less than $100 per month. As this income is included in total survivor income (Table 4-5), it is not analyzed independently.

Immediate Adjustment Expenses

As a charge against the death-created resources, the survivor must somehow meet the special expenses that accrue in conjunction with the death of the worker.

Table 4-5

Survivor Family Income[a]

	1963	1965
	(%)	(%)
N =	287	361
< $1000	12%	4%
$1000 - 1999	19	16
2000 - 2999	16	16
3000 - 3999	15	13
4000 - 4999	14	14
5000 - 5999	10	9
6000 - 6999	7	9
7000 - 7999	3	8
8000 - 8999	1	4
9000 +	4	8
Median	$3250	$4140

[a]Income from all sources; 1965 income is a 12-month projection based on figures obtained at interview.

For purposes of this study, such costs are referred to as Immediate Adjustment Expenses. In the language of the insurance industry, similar cost concepts are variously referred to as cleanup funds, probate funds, or estate clearance funds. They consist specifically of (1) unpaid hospital, physicians, and similar medical bills incident to the worker's last illness; (2) burial expenses, including funeral costs, cemetery lot, markers, and so on; (3) personal obligations, including unpaid notes, personal loans, installment payments, and other unsatisfied accounts; (4) unpaid pledges; (5) cost of estate administration, including executors' or administrators' fees, court costs, legal fees, and appraisers' fees; and (6) estate, inheritance, income, and property taxes.

In this section all initial adjustment costs described above are discussed, with the exception of funeral costs. (Funeral costs are discussed in Chapter 5). However, funeral costs are included when total immediate adjustment costs are reported. Debts, which many consider to be an immediate survivor expense, are not included in total immediate adjustment costs for the purposes of the present analysis. Rather, they are compared to assets on the assumption that many debts are not called on the worker's death. Moreover, it was recognized that debts would first be a charge against assets, if any, before payment was made, often out of lump sum resources existing before the worker's death or created as a result of such death.

Medical Expenses. In the vast majority of the cases involving dependent survivors, the hospital and medical charges payable after the death of the workers were insignificant relative to the survivors' total immediate adjustment costs. Fifty-eight percent of the 1963 survivors and 57% of the 1965 survivors had no hospital charges at all. And 34% of the 1963 group and 33% of the 1965 group had hospital charges due that were less than $100. Only 1% in 1963 and one person in 1965 had due hospital expenses that may be considered catastrophic, that is, over $800.

No 1963 survivors reported medical payments of this magnitude as due. Similarly low due charges for doctor bills were reported for 1965 survivors. Two-thirds of all dependent survivors reported no medical charges due after the worker's death. When such charges were due, however, they tended in two out of three cases to be under $100.

Charges for other medical expenses were even less prevalent. For the two years combined, only 25 dependent survivors reported any expense for nursing care; 35 for medicines, and 2 for nursing home care. Of the total number (62) reporting such expenses, two-thirds (41) reported that these charges were less than $100. The only unusual charges were two cases in which special nursing costs of $825 and $1400 were reported.

When all postdeath due charges in the above health care categories are totaled, only 25% of the cases in 1963 and 23% in 1965 reported charges that exceeded $100. 37% in 1963 and 33% in 1965 reported no due charges for all health care received by the deceased worker.

The low charges due for medical care are to be expected since the workers covered were considered to have among the best health care coverage then available in Michigan and the United States as a result of collectively bargained health insurance. In applying the findings regarding immediate and ongoing adequacy to other groups, these low charges apparently resulting from relatively high quality health insurance must be borne in mind. No evidence on health care costs incurred and paid by the individual or family prior to the worker's death is available. However, to the extent that these were significant, they would be reflected in a reduced level of savings reported by the family for the period prior to the worker's death and at interview.

Eighty-two percent of the dependent surviving units reported that they retained some form of health insurance protection, often paid for through the husband's former employer. Approximately 5% of those covered, (the same percentage of coverage reported prior to the worker's death) retained group coverage with Community Health Association; 87% were covered by Blue Cross. The remainder reported other coverages.[c]

As a result of the 1967 Big Three Auto Agreements, widows of workers eligible to retire when they died are now entitled to company-paid health insurance protection.

Estate Administration and Taxes. Due to the relatively small estates, the number of survivors who had to pay inheritance taxes on the deceased worker's estate was negligible; only 3% in both years. The amount of taxes accrued varied from $1 to $455 in 1963 and from $13 to $753 in 1965.

The cost of estate administration, and other cleanup legal expenses, was also relatively low as a whole. In the main, these expenses were attorney's fees. Twenty-two percent of the dependent survivors in 1963 and 26% in 1965 had expenses in this category. The highest expenses in this category were associated with liability suits where the worker died in an accident. (Spot checking of probate records generally confirmed the accuracy of information reported on this topic.)

Total Costs of Immediate Adjustment. The total costs of the dependent survivor's initial adjustment were, exclusive of debt, virtually identical in the two study years. In making these comparisons, as before, the median is used to measure central tendency.

The median group life insurance benefit, (reported above and in Chapter 5) for dependent survivors was approximately $7000 (slightly less in 1963). There were 17 cases above $10,000. The median immediate adjustment costs for both study years were about $1700 and only three cases are observed that exceeded

[c]In Michigan in 1965, 89% of the population had hospital coverage, 86% (surgical) and 73% (medical). *Statistical Abstract of the United States,* 1967, Table 672. Though no figures are available, it is assumed that a lesser percentage of the general survivor population had such coverage.

Table 4-6

**Total Immediate Cost of Dependent
Survivor Adjustment[a]
(% Distribution)**

Immediate Adjustment Cost		1963	1965
	N=	331	389
Under $1000		5%	4%
$1000-$1499		36	31
1500- 1999		31	37
2000- 2499		17	18
2500- 2999		4	5
3000 and over		6	6
		100%**	100%**
Median		$1640	$1700

[a]Funeral costs, estate administration and
taxes, and medical expenses payable after
the worker's death.
**May not add due to rounding.

the $10,000 amount. If debt (nonmortgage) is included, median immediate
adjustment costs for both years rises to approximately $2100.

Thus, it is apparent that in the aggregate at least, group life insurance
proceeds more than met immediate adjustment expenses as defined in this study.
If total insurance proceeds were compared to death related expenses, the
apparent disparity would be even greater. This is further considered in the next
section in connection with the problems of ongoing adjustment.

Group insurance proceeds were not individually compared with initial
adjustment expenses as such programs are not generally tailored to individual
needs. Again, it must be borne in mind that these survivors faced relatively low
postdeath medical expenses.

Ongoing Adequacy of Survivor Benefits

As has been shown, the negotiated group insurance proceeds have generally met the total immediate adjustment costs and provided some additional protection to the surviving family. A broader measure of adequacy is required, however, to evaluate the short and long run effectiveness of all of the elements of survivor benefits.

Survivor Financial Position

As a broad indicator of ongoing adequacy, the DCWFB score projected at the time of interview is used. For the 1963 group, the relatively long run ongoing adjustment had apparently not been generally successful, in that 48% of the widow-headed dependent survivor units fell more than $500 below the DCWFB standard. The shorter run (overall) adjustment for many of the 1965 group was similarly less than satisfactory, (35% failed to meet the standard) but this may reflect the period of reduced standard of living which may be expected in the case of death of the breadwinner. (Table 4-7). The 35% failure to meet the DCWFB standard is particularly significant when it is recalled that nearly nine out of ten of the 1965 survivors were already receiving the Transition Benefit ($100 per month) at the time of their interview.

In analyzing the ongoing adjustment, age of widow, size of family, receipt of Social Security, and work status of family members were specifically considered. Table 4-8 summarizes these data. DCWFB scores respond as might be expected, *a priori*. However, size of family does not seem systematically related to DCWFB score. A major generalization that emerges from studying 4-8 is that substantial numbers in nearly each category considered failed to meet the DCWFB standard of a modest but adequate level of living.

For the 1963 group of survivors, the above DCWFB figures do include the impact of employment earnings, if any, for widows and other dependents. As indicated in Chapter 3, a higher percentage of auto worker surviving widows are employed than of United States widows in general.

The percentage of wives employed after the worker's death increased substantially for the 1963 survivors and somewhat less for the 1965 group. While 22% of the 1963 wives were working full time at the time of their husband's death and 10% worked part time; at the time of interview, these figures had increased to 33% and 18% (see Table 4-13 for a summary of this income).

Thus, assuming no change in Social Security earnings rulings, unless wage income can be improved either by training for better jobs or a general wage increase or as additional dependents enter the labor market (or nonwage earning dependents leave home), the only source of upgrading the financial status of the average dependent surviving family unit is improved public or private survivor benefits.

The 1965 survivors had not generally turned to work as an adjustment to the husband's death to the extent that the 1963 survivors had. In part, this reflects

Table 4-7

**Dependent Survivor Family Financial
Status[a] (% Distribution)**

Financial Status	1963	1965
N=	287	361
Below DCWFB		
$2,000 (or more)	18%	9%
1,000 - $1,999	20	18
500 - 999	10	8
DCWFB ± $500	18	19
Above DCWFB		
$ 500 - $ 999	5	6
1,000 - . 1,999	12	11
2,000 - 2,999	8	11
3,000 - 3,999	4	7
4,000 (and more)	4	10
	100%**	100%**

[a]A comparison of reported family income
(adjusted to an annual basis) and the
DCWFB budget adjusted to reflect 1966
prices. Excludes families headed by a widow
who has remarried and those families for
which an accurate income estimate could
not be obtained.
**May not add due to rounding.

the shorter adjustment period considered for the 1965 group. In addition, the 1965 group had relatively younger children which further limits work as an adjustment. The 1965 group was receiving the Transition Benefit and those dependent widows over 50 at the time of their husband's death will receive the Bridge Benefit. Given the limited adjustment period considered for this group, it was not possible to evaluate the impact of these benefits.

The survivor's adjustment may be seen in a broader perspective by

Table 4-8

**Financial Position and Selected
Variables (% Distribution)[a]**

	Age of Widow at Interview							
	35-49		*50-61*		62-64		65+	
	1963	*1965*	*1963*	*1965*	*1963*	*1965*	*1963*	*1965*
N=	69	115	160	165	28	29	22	19
% Below DCWFB[b]	54%	34%	45%	41%	57%	20%	40%	15%
% DCWFB[c]	7	13	22	22	18	38	27	21
% Above DCWFB	39%	53%	33%	37%	25%	42%	33%	64%

	Cause of Worker's Death			
	Illness		Accident	
	1963	*1965*	*1963*	*1965*
N=	268	323	19	38
% Below DCWFB	50%	36%	22%	29%
% DCWFB ± $500	17	21	26	8
% Above DCWFB	34%	42%	51%	63%

	Widow's Work Status at Interview					
	Full Time		Part Time		Not Working	
	1963	*1965*	*1963*	*1965*	*1963*	*1965*
N=	96	84	49	35	138	234
% Below DCWFB	9%	2%	51%	26%	74%	47%
% DCWFB ± $500	21	5	20	14	15	26
% Above DCWFB	70%	93%	28%	59%	12%	27%

Table 4-8 (continued)

	Number of Nonwidow Working Dependents					
	None		One		Two +	
	1963	*1965*	*1963*	*1965*	*1963*	*1965*
N=	119	222	136	121	34	18
% Below DCWFB	89%	70%	41%	23%	33%	45%
% DCWFB ± $500	5	20	21	12	24	17
% Above DCWFB	7%	9%	38%	65%	45%	50%

	Receipt of Social Security			
	Yes		No	
	1963	*1965*	*1963*	*1965*
N=	136	174	151	186
Below DCWFB	51%	25%	38%	43%
DCWFB ± $500	18	22	18	17
Above DCWFB	30%	53%	44%	40%

	Age of Dependents			
	Under 13		13-21	
	1963	*1965*	*1963*	*1965*
N= (Number of Units)	23	34	96	89
Below DCWFB	48%	26%	49%	33%
DCWFB ± $500	17	21	35	16
Above DCWFB	35%	53%	15%	50%

Table 4-8 (continued)

	Size of Family							
	One		Two		Three		Four +	
	1963	1965	1963	1965	1963	1965	1963	1965
N=	145	170	50	77	39	49	41	55
Below DCWFB	35%	36%	34%	23%	34%	23%	32%	49%
DCWFB ± $500	19	22	20	23	21	23	10	5
Above DCWFB	46%	42%	46%	53%	45%	53%	58%	45%

[a]May not add to 100%.

[b]Below or Above DCWFB is defined as income more than $500 below or above this standard.

[c]DCWFB includes those up to $500 or less above or below the DCWFB standard (see Table B-3 for DCWFB standards).

Note: For the entire group (for whom data are available) of dependent widow-headed survivor units:

	1963	1965
N=	283	353
%Below DCWFB	48%	34%
%DCWFB	18	20
% Above DCWFB	34%	46%

considering a profile of those widow-headed survivor units whose income failed to meet the DCWFB standard by more than $500. Table 4-9 summarizes major characteristics of survivor groups $500 (or more) above or below the DCWFB standard. Thus, 50% of those widow-headed units falling more than $500 below the DCWFB standard in 1963 were widow-only units; a percentage comparable to that in the total sample.

More than one out of four of those units that failed to meet the DCWFB standard by $500 or more (1963) reported no group insurance proceeds retained at the time of the interview. Only one out of ten of these survivors could draw on retained group insurance proceeds of $5000 or more. Though no specific question was asked about overall savings, more than eight out of ten dependent survivors reported no or negligible interest income, confirming the general lack of savings that might supplement deficient incomes.

Table 4-9

**Selected Characteristics of Dependent
Survivor Units Above or Below DCWFB
Standard**

	1963		1965	
Characteristic	% $500 (and more) Above DCWFB	% $500 (and more) Below DCWFB	% $500 (and more) Above DCWFB	% $500 (and more) Below DCWFB
Size of unit—one person	53%	44%	50%	52%
Widows Age				
45-54	44	45	39	43
55-64	36	23	39	32
Widows Work Status— not working	16	40	75	91
Race—Non-Caucasian	12	17	28	29
Widow Education— <8th grade	34	25	40	45
Home Ownership—Yes	82	88	72	77
Group Insurance Proceeds Retained—				
None	24	12	28	16
$5000 (and more)	21	43	12	27

The characteristics of those widow-headed survivor units whose income exceeded the DCWFB standard by $500 or more differ markedly from those having lower DCWFB scores. For example, while 75% of the 1963 widows whose income failed to meet the DCWFB standard were not working, only 16% of those whose income exceeded this standard were not employed. A similar contrast is evident in considering race. Caucasians constituted 72% of the 1963 surviving units below the DCWFB standard and 88% of those above the standard. (78% of the workers leaving dependent survivors were Caucasian).

A direct contrast between surviving units above and below the DCWFB standard is provided in Table 4-10 for several major characteristics of survivors. In evaluating these data, the stage of adjustment must be considered as the relationship of the variables is seldom consistent for the two years studied. Thus, 21% of those 1963 survivors whose incomes placed them $500 or more above

Table 4-10

DCWFB Score Comparison of Selected Characteristics (Widow-Headed Survivor Units)[a]

			Worker Skill Category	
	N	*I*	*II*	*III*
$500 + above[b]				
1963	97	40%	27%	33%
1965	163	44%	24%	32%
$500 + below				
1963	135	36%	36%	28%
1965	120	52%	25%	23%

			Size of Family		
	N	*1*	*2*	*3*	*4 +*
$500 + above					
1963	97	53%	21%	13%	13%
1965	163	44%	25%	15%	16%
$500 + below					
1963	135	50%	20%	13%	17%
1965	120	52%	15%	11%	22%

				Group Insurance Proceeds Retained			
	N	*None*	*< $1000*	*$1000 - 1999*	*$2000 - 2999*	*$3000 - 3999*	*$4000 - 4999*	*$5000+*
$500 + above								
1963	86	26%	6%	14%	9%	11%	12%	21%
1965	148	13%	6%	4%	9%	13%	11%	43%
$500 + below								
1963	128	28%	13%	12%	9%	14%	11%	12%
1965	109	16%	4%	10%	15%	10%	18%	27%

[a]Widow-headed families for whom data are available: (N = 287 - 1963; 361 - 1965)

	$500 + above DCWFB	*$500 + below DCWFB*
1963	34%	48%
1965	46%	35%

[b]Cutoff figures indicate $500 + above or below DCWFB standard indicated in Table B-3.

the DCWFB standard had retained $5000 or more group insurance proceeds at the time of the interview. Twenty-seven percent of the 1965 survivors $500 or more below the DCWFB standard reported this amount of group insurance proceeds retained. Furthermore, while more than half of the 1965 survivors whose income left them more than $500 below the DCWFB standard had a substantial potential amount of resources to draw on ($3000 or more group insurance proceeds retained); less than 40 percent of the 1963 survivors in this DCWFB category could draw on a similar amount of resources.

The differential rate of depletion of resources over time (1963 vs. 1965 survivors) is further indicated by these data. While it is impossible (with the present data) to know precisely the amounts of actual resources available to meet demonstrated deficiencies in the "modest but adequate" DCWFB budget

Table 4-11

Postfatality Family Income[a]

	1963		1965	
	%	*Cumulative %*	*%*	*Cumulative %*
N =	287		361	
< $1000	12%	12%	4%	4%
$1000 - 1999	19	31	16	20
2000 - 2999	16	47	16	36
3000 - 3999	14	62	13	49
4000 - 4999	14	76	14	63
5000 - 5999	10	86	9	72
6000 - 6999	7	93	9	81
8000 - 8999	1	97	4	93
9000 +	4	100**	8	100**
Median	$3250		$4140	

[a]Income from all sources; 1965 income is a 12-month projection based on figures obtained at interview.

**Rounding error.

standard, all evidence indicates that any remaining liquid "capital" represents at best a very limited potential resource for a minority of those with low DCWFB scores.

Survivor Income and Adjustment

Further insight regarding the survivor's adjustment problems may be obtained by examining the distribution of post-death income. Median post-death income of

Table 4-12

Monthly Social Security Benefits[a]
(% Distribution)

	1963		1965	
	% of Dep.	% of Soc. Sec. Beneficiaries	% of Dep.	% of Soc. Sec. Beneficiaries
N =	340	166	395	197
50 - $ 99	10%	20%	7%	14%
100 - 149	14	28	11	23
150 - 199	10	22	10	20
200 - 249	1	2	3	6
250 - 299	10	20	11	21
300 +	2	5	7	14
No Answer	1	2	1	1
No Benefit	51	-	50	-
	100%	100%**	100%	100%**
Median (with benefit)	$152		$183[b]	

[a]Dependent survivors only; includes all recipients among surviving unit.

[b]Includes relatively higher percent of family benefits.

**Rounding error.

Table 4-13

**Sources of Dependent Survivor
Family Weekly Income
(% Distribution)** **

				Weekly Income				
Income Source		N	Under $20	$20-49	$50-99	$100 & Over	Median	% Without Income[a]
Widow Work	1963	158	11%	25%	48%	15%	$64	54%
	1965	119	8	22	40	30	66	70
Other Work	1963	54	30	42	17	11	34	84
	1965	51	43	43	10	4	25	87
Gifts	1963	24	38	25	4	33	35	93
	1965	20	45	40	10	5	24	95
Rental & Other	1963	135	52	34	11	2	19	60
	1965	179	36	48	12	5	29	55
Total Weekly Income[b]	1963	271	16	28	36	20	58	20
	1965	296	22	31	28	19	47	25
Interest Income		N	$1<3	$3<6	$6<10	$10 & Over	Median	% without Income
	1963	51	27%	31%	20%	22%	$ 4	85
	1965	76	16	34	25	24	5	81

[a]% of all dependent survivors (340 - - 1963, 395 - - 1965) without income from indicated source.

[b]Includes interest income (whole dollar amounts only). If less than $0.50 per week interest income was reported, it was coded as None.

**May not add due to rounding.

the 1963 survivors was $3250; this compares to the pre-death median family income for this group of $6900 (Table 3-16), a drop of more than 50%. For the 1965 survivors, median post-death income was $4140 as compared with $7410.

Over 60% of the dependent survivors (both years) had applied for Social Security benefits. Eighty percent of those who had applied (363) were receiving such benefits at the time of their interview. As might be expected, a somewhat lower percentage of the 1965 beneficiaries had applied for Social Security benefits (less time since death); however, a higher percentage of that year's survivors were receiving benefits at the time of interview. This latter finding is confirmed by the presence of more wage earners in the 1963 survivor group and of more young children in the 1965 group.

The above is consistent with data and *a priori* expectations. Twenty-three percent of the 1963 widows were over 60 at the time of the interview. Moreover, in the two or more years since the 1963 deaths, relatively more widows had returned to work and relatively more children passed the age of dependency.

Social Security monthly income for the group studied ranged from $50 to over $400 for all members of the surviving unit receiving such benefits. Table 4-12 summarizes the monthly benefits, which include benefits received by dependent parents. Such benefits are not subject to the Social Security family maximum. Social Security benefits are not taxable.

In addition to the above resources created by the worker's death, the beneficiaries supplemented their income by working and some received gifts. Table 4-13 summarizes these sources. There were five (under 1%) reports of survivors receiving public assistance (included in rental and other income); however, this question was not asked specifically. The presence of significant cash resources disqualifies a family or individual from receipt of welfare payments. In addition, for most family sizes the DCWFB budget standard is somewhat higher than that applied to welfare recipients. Thus, a family could fail to meet the DCWFB standard for a modest but adequate level of living and still not qualify for the receipt of public assistance.

Independent of Social Security and the negotiated Transition benefit (1965 survivors) the greatest single source of income was widows working. Other dependents also contributed work income. A significant percent of dependent survivor units reported interest income—15% (1963) and 19% (1965). While most survivors reported no interest income, for those who reported such income, indicated investments (4% interest assumed) ranged from $1250 to over $37,000. The higher amounts were associated with accidental death settlements or inheritances.

Survivor Assets and Debts

The large number reporting no investments (no interest) and the small amounts of cash inferred from the interest income reported lead the authors to conclude that the use of cash assets to meet the shortfall indicated when income was compared to the DCWFB standard is not likely to be a significant source of upgrading. Moreover, given the characteristics of those failing to meet the DCWFB standard, it is apparent (Table 4-10) that many do not have cash savings to draw upon. Finally, the assumption appears tenable that whatever cash and other assets remain are first used to meet debt obligations left by the worker.

As may be noted in Table 4-14, which follows, there were more survivors with loans and other personal obligations outstanding in 1963 than 1965. Thirty percent reported owing some money in 1963 and only 17% had this kind of obligation in 1965. This may be partially explained by the observation that 1965 was a better year than 1963 for auto production. Moreover, 1965 followed several years of relatively full employment. In addition, credit was more difficult and expensive to obtain in 1965, and this may also partially explain the difference shown. No attempt was made to compare these debt figures to those for other populations.

The difficulty of *a priori* explanations of the above phenomenon is indicated by the observation that the 1965 survivors who were in debt owed more (higher median) than survivors in 1963.

When survivors were asked to identify the creditors for the above obligations, 46% reported banking institutions. Thirty-nine percent reported loan companies and only 14% reported credit unions—of any kind. The numbers of those reporting in each year are too small to allow the researchers to generalize about trends in worker borrowing behavior between the two study years.

The most frequently reported uses of these loans were for items related to the worker's household needs. Automobile purchases were second in importance. Only nine cases in both years combined reported obligations due to school tuition. The uses of the group insurance proceeds by the survivors are reported in Chapter 5.

Considering all assets and debts at the time of the worker's death (excluding value of house and mortgage payable) more than 3 out of 5 had positive assets. For most, however, such net assets amounted to less than $2,000. Moreover, even if total assets only are considered, the picture of limited resources available to meet income deficiencies is largely confirmed. As indicated in Table 4-16, approximately two out of three dependent surviving units reported total assets (savings, securities, property and business interests) of less than $3,000.

Thus, it is apparent that the ongoing adjustment problems of the group of survivors studied, particularly the 1963 group of survivors are significant. In more personal terms, these problems are indicated in the fact that 27% of the 1963 survivors reported changing their residence since their husband's death. Of greater significance, perhaps, 42% of these reported that they had moved for financial reasons. An additional group reported moving back home so that the widow's parents could help care for the children. More than one in four (1963) and one in three (1965) of the survivors reported cutting back on living expenses following the death of the workers. (This difference cannot be explained.) Of these, the greatest single adjustment was in reduced quantity or quality of food or clothing (60%). Other major cutbacks were reported in entertainment and

Table 4-14[a]

Debts Payable at Workers' Death

Debts	1963	1965
N =	101	69
< $ 500	38%	23%
$ 500 - $ 900	28	26
1000 - 1499	18	12
1500 - 1999	10	12
2000 - 2499	2	9
2500 +	5	19
	100%**	100%**
Median debt	$732	$1263
% reporting debt	30%	17%

[a]Dependent survivors; excludes mortgages and other debts on tangible assets.
**Rounding error.

shelter. While adjustments by survivors are generally anticipated, these changes indicate the depth and breadth of the adjustment made by survivors of the workers studied.

Knowledge of Benefit Plans

Another dimension in evaluating the adequacy of survivor benefits, is the survivor's knowledge of such benefits. For both years, 4% of the survivors reported that they did not apply for the lump sum Social Security burial benefit. Less than 1% of those survivors eligible for monthly benefits failed to apply for them because they didn't need or believe in the benefits.

Nearly 50% of the survivors reported that they had received some help (by the mortician in 61% of the cases where help was received), in applying for Social Security benefits. Only 4 of the 351 who received help in filing for

Table 4-15[a]

Net Asset–Debt Position
(% Distribution)

	1963		1965	
	%	*Cumulative %*	*%*	*Cumulative %*
N =	319		373	
Debt				
$3000 +	4%	4%	4%	4%
2000 - $2999	4	8	1	5
1000 - 1999	8	16	9	14
001 - 999	21	37	20	34
Assets				
$ 001 - $ 999	28	65	25	59
1000 - 1999	7	72	7	66
2000 - 2999	4	76	6	72
3000 - 5999	11	87	13	85
6000 +	14	100**	16	100**

[a]Excludes value of house and amount owed; dependent survivors at death; excludes those for whom data are incomplete.
**Rounding error.

benefits reported a specific charge for such help, though for some the charge may have been hidden. Twenty-nine percent of those with benefits in addition to the deceased worker's group life insurance reported assistance in filing for such benefits. Only 12 of the 171 who had such benefits (7%) reported a charge (usually by an attorney) for such assistance. This is elaborated in Chapter 6.

The information gap with respect to the group life insurance benefits is indicated by the fact that 41 dependent beneficiaries out of 735 (6%) could not accurately report the amount of their lump sum benefit. An additional 29

Table 4-16

**Family Financial Resources at
Worker's Death**[a]
(% Distribution)

	1963		1965	
	%	*Cumulative %*	*%*	*Cumulative %*
N =	322		376	
None	30%	30%	26%	26%
< $1000	29	59	28	54
$1000 - $1999	10	69	8	62
2000 - 2999	5	74	8	70
3000 - 3999	5	79	6	76
4000 - 4999	3	82	4	80
5000 - 5999	4	86	3	83
6000 - 9999	6	92	6	89
10,000 + [b]	8	100	11	100
Median	$690		$860	

[a]Includes value of savings, securities,
property, and interest in a business.
  Excludes families with incomplete data.
[b]Ranges to $74,000.

beneficiaries would not reply. Further, while 97% of the dependent survivors took a lump sum benefit, only 38% of the beneficiaries reported that they knew they could choose between lump sum and monthly benefits. A variety of reasons were given for the choice of a lump sum benefit. Twenty-two percent of those who were unaware of their option, however, reported that they would have chosen monthly installments had they known of this alternative.

The Transition and Bridge benefits, inaugurated in the 1964 auto contracts, were too new, perhaps, for the 1965 survivors to be expected to have adequate knowledge of them. Still, nearly three-fourths of the 1965 widows, aged 50-60 at the time of the worker's death, did not expect or did not know about receiving the Bridge benefit. Knowledge was similarly limited regarding its amount and the duration of payment.

In summary then, for both groups of survivors studied, the potential ability of the worker's group survivor benefits to meet immediate adjustment expenses has been demonstrated. However, serious doubt has been cast as to the ability of such benefits to provide a substantial proportion of the surviving dependent family units with a modest but adequate ongoing standard of living, even in conjunction with work and other adjustments. Knowledge of group and other survivor benefits is mixed. Improvement here would be a useful step toward upgrading the efficacy of survivor benefits overall.

5 Utilization of Group Life Insurance Proceeds

In judging the adequacy and efficacy of the survivors's group life insurance proceeds in the overall context of all survivor benefits, specific consideration of the uses of these insurance proceeds is essential. Even with such consideration, however, the question of adequacy cannot formally be resolved except with reference to the norms of the society or an agreed upon standard, such as the DCWFB.

An additional factor complicating the evaluation of survivor benefits overall is the limited knowledge of such benefits by the beneficiaries as was indicated in Chapter 4. Moreover, it is difficult to evaluate one survivor benefit component when the overall benefits are seldom (and often are too inflexible to be) coordinated by the providing agencies or counselors for the recipients. Such coordination (and possibly greater overall benefit flexibility) might bring the existing complex of benefits closer to functioning as an interrelated program rather than as fragmented dollar and service benefits.

As discussed in Chapter 4, dependent survivors received an average of $6500 to $7000 in lump sum life insurance proceeds—representing for the great majority of families (in all probability) an unprecedently large sum of immediately disposable cash. The range in specific amounts is shown in Table 5-1. Less than 2% of all survivors, as noted earlier, elected an option to receive this resource, in whole or in part, in monthly installments. Two 1965 dependent survivor units reported that they had not received any group life insurance payment—possibly due to recency of death and incompletion of claim identification and processing. All but three of the recipients of lump sum payments reported funeral expenditures as one major use of insurance proceeds.[b]

---

[a]Except as noted, expenditures refer to dependent survivor-beneficiaries (Long Form). Selected tables refer to widow-headed surviving units only. Funeral expenditures and insurance proceeds by nondependent survivors are also reported separately.

[b]Respondents were generally willing and able to report extensively on the uses of the group insurance proceeds which they had (conceptually at least) segregated from other cash resources or income generated by the worker's death. The accuracy of some of the expenditure data (for example, burial costs, attorney's fees) was verified by checking probate records for a nonrandom group of respondents. The willingness to talk about uses of segregated amounts of money was also reported in a confidential study of survivors made available to the authors by a major insurance company. This willingness by respondents in the present study may be attributable to the care with which they were approached for an interview and the repeated assurance of confidentiality. As mentioned in the methodological appendix, the UAW cooperated (at all levels) in encouraging beneficiaries to participate fully in the study. There is some indication, however, that income figures may have been overstated by some respondents. This must be noted in interpreting the adequacy of income and related issues.

Table 5-1

Lump Sum Proceeds from Worker's Group Life Insurance (% Distribution)

$ Proceeds[a]	1963		
	Nondep.	*Dep.*	*Dep. & Nondep.*
N =	69	340	409
%N =	17%	83%	100%
$1000-$4999	7%	2%	3%
5000- 5999	12	7	8
6000- 6999	61	59	59
7000- 7999	14	9	10
8000- 8999	4	19	16
9000+	1	3	3
Not applicable[b]	*	1	1
	100%**	100%**	100%
Mean	$6370[c]	$6840	$6760
Median	$6520	$6700	$6660
	1965		
N =	69	395	464
%N =	15%	85%	100%
$1000-$4999	3%	*	1%
5000- 5999	1	*	1
6000- 6999	59	45%	47
7000- 7999	22	24	23
8000- 8999	7	19	17
9000+	6	8	8
Not applicable[b]	1	3	3
	100%**	100%**	100%
Mean	$6830	$7150	$7100
Median	$6780	$7160	$7050

Table 5-1 (continued)

	1963 & 1965		
N =	138	735	873
%N =	16%	84%	100%
$1000-$4999	5%	1%	2%
5000- 5999	6	4	4
6000- 6999	60	52	53
7000- 7999	18	17	17
8000- 8999	6	19	17
9000+	4	6	5
Not applicable[b]	1	2	2
	100%**	100%**	100%
Mean	$6600	$7010	$6940
Median	$6640	$6880	$6840

[a]Includes Accidental Death and Disability benefits. A totally and permanently disabled worker may, under the negotiated contract, draw payment of his basic life insurance amount while living, the remainder to be paid on his death. Even if the total amount is drawn, a $500 burial benefit is paid.

[b]Includes those taking monthly installments and those reporting no benefits. For discussion of these cases, see text.

[c]Rounded to nearest $10.00—as are all income data unless noted otherwise.

*Less than 0.6%.

**Rounding error.

*, Typically, choices with respect to funeral arrangements and the amount to be expended for this purpose are the first to confront survivors following a breadwinner's death and may require decision even before the exact extent of other immediate postdeath expenses are fully known. Funeral costs are analyzed in the first section of this chapter; and the implied residual survivor benefit and other uses of the lump sum benefit are considered in the second.

Expenditures on Worker's Funeral

Funeral Costs

Table 5-2 summarizes the cost of workers' funerals. Selected statistics on these funerals are indicated in Table 5-3, which is discussed further, below. Funeral costs in the two study years remained relatively constant and were greatly in excess of the $255 maximum lump sum burial benefit paid under Social Security. Total costs reported by dependent survivors ranged (1963) from $40 to $4411, with median of $1490; and (1965) from $518 to $4220 with a median of $1550. Funeral costs reported by nondependent survivors varied similarly. In 1963, these costs ranged between $601 and $3397 with a median of $1620; and in 1965, such costs ranged between $650 and $6000 with a median of $1570.

Three additional points must be considered in comparing funeral costs (Table 5-3):

1. the variability of the component charges between 1963 and 1965;
2. the high proportion of respondents unable to itemize funeral charges—531 of the 868 actually reporting funeral charges (61%) could not itemize such charges;
3. the difference between undertaker charges when not itemized and the average total cost for all funerals. Either individuals not able to itemize failed to report all charges or the cost of package funerals is lower. It is not possible to substantiate either interpretation.

The price variability and lack of price information suggests some of the difficulties faced by survivors as they arrange for the worker's funeral.

Median funeral costs for major survivor groups are summarized in Table 5-4. It is noted that the median cost generally increased (but by less than the U.S. Consumer Price Index) between 1963 and 1965. The cost reported by nondependent beneficiaries and surviving families with no widow declined somewhat between the two years. In view of the small number of cases involved and the relatively small decline, these variations were not analyzed independently.

Table 5-2

Funeral Cost
(% Distribution)

Total Cost	1963	1965	1963 & 1965
	Dependent Survivors		
N =	340	395	735
1-$ 500	1%	*	*
500- 749	2	2%	2%
750- 999	5	7	6
1000- 1249	19	17	18
1250- 1499	24	21	22
1500- 1749	19	24	21
1750- 1999	12	12	12
2000- 2249	9	9	9
2250- 2499	3	4	4
2500- 2749	3	3	3
2750- 4500	3	2	2
Don't know	1	*	*
% of Survivors	100%**	100%**	100%**
Mean[a]	$1560	$1590 (+ 2%)[b]	$1580
Median[a]	$1490	$1550 (+ 4%)[b]	$1520
	Nondependent Survivors		
N =	69	69	138
$ 500-$ 999	4%	7%	6%
1000- 1499	36	38	37
1500- 1999	42	39	40
2000- 2499	14	12	13
2500- 2999	1	1	1
3000- 6000	1	3	2
% of Survivors	100%**	100%	100%**
Mean[a]	$1640	$1650 (+ 1%)[b]	$1640
Median[a]	$1620	$1570 (− 3%)[b]	$1590
	Dependent and Nondependent Survivors		
Mean[a]	$1580	$1600 (+ 1%)[b]	$1590
Median[a]	$1520	$1560 (+ 3%)[b]	$1540

[a]Rounded to nearest $10.
[b]% change 1963 to 1965.
*Less than 0.6%
**Rounding error

Table 5-3

**Selected Statistics on the Cost of
Worker's Funeral**

Dependent Survivors

1963

Items	Number Reporting Cost	Cost Range	Median[b]
Cost of Casket	96	$350-$1500	$ 875
Burial Vault	84	35- 2500	130
Cemetery charges	162	10- 690	150
Grave marker	195	12- 700	140
Honorariums	145	5- 200	25
Transportation	32	8- 1029	40
Mortician charges	67	19- 1890	380
Undertaker's bill[a]	218	10- 3800	1200
Other charges	206	3- 1350	65
	338	$ 40-$4411	$1490

	1965			% Change (Median Cost) 1963-65
Cost of casket	141	$ 6-$1900	$ 860	− 2%
Burial Vault	150	30- 3000	145	+ 12
Cemetery charges	208	10- 650	150	N.C.
Grave marker	214	20- 1000	150	+ 7
Honorariums	186	5- 175	25	N.C.
Transportation	42	9- 225	50	+ 19
Mortician charges	101	10- 1778	440	+ 15
Undertaker's bill[a]	213	28- 3000	1200	N.C.
Other charges	271	4- 596	70	+ 3
	394	$518-$4220	$1550	+ 4

Table 5-3 (continued)

Nondependent Survivors

1963

	Number Reporting Cost	*Cost Range*	*Median* [b]
Cost of casket	21	$750-$1350	$1000
Burial Vault	21	75- 500	150
Cemetery charges	29	25- 1315	125
Grave marker	35	30- 609	135
Honorariums	32	10- 100	25
Transportation	6	25- 240	100
Mortician charges	13	103- 1900	505
Undertaker's bill[a]	44	500- 2000	1270
Other charges	39	1- 795	135
	69	$601-$3397	$1620

	1965			*% Change (Median Cost) 1963-65*
Cost of casket	20	$500-$1204	$ 955	− 4%
Burial Vault	18	35- 300	150	N.C.
Cemetery Charges	29	25- 399	130	+ 4
Grave marker	29	8- 800	140	+ 2
Honorariums	29	10- 95	25	N.C.
Transportation	6	15- 270	90	− 10
Mortician charges	12	35- 1685	255	− 50
Undertaker's bill[a]	46	650- 5700	1300	+ 2
Other charges	31	1- 825	70	− 47
	69	$650-$6000	$1570	−3%

N.C. - No Change

[a]Respondents who could not itemize were requested to indicate total undertaker's bill here.

[b]Median data are rounded to nearest $5.

Table 5-4

**Median Total Funeral Cost for
Selected Survivor Characteristics[a]**

Survivor Characteristics	1963		1965		1963-1965
	Number	Median	Number	Median	% Change
Dependent Survivors	340	$1490	395	$1550	+ 4%
Nondependent Survivors Only	69	1620	69	1570	- 3
All Workers	409	1520	464	1560	+ 3
Widow Survivors	325	1500	367	1580	+ 5
No Widow Survivor	15	1340	28	1290	- 5

[a]Rounded to nearest $10.

Elements of Total Funeral Cost

Respondents to the survey instruments were asked to report in detail on the various elements which constituted the total funeral cost that they experienced. It was considered desirable to collect such detailed information for three reasons:

1. to isolate specific items in order to identify those that represent major elements of expense;
2. as a field device, such isolation served to assist respondents in their ability to recall all elements of expense if receipts were not obtainable;
3. in consideration of the apparent lack of detailed information of this nature in the literature, it is felt that other interested researchers may find this detail of some value.

In all cases (for survivors who could itemize costs) the most costly item of funeral expense was the cost of the casket. Second only to the cost of the casket were the mortician charges. It is of particular interest to observe that for nondependent beneficiaries (Short Form) the median cost of the casket was typically higher (a difference of $125 in 1963; $95 in 1965) then casket costs for workers who were survived by dependents. Several possible explanations may be offered, but it is impossible to reliably explain this finding.

Table 5-5

Summary Comparative Funeral Costs

Estimate	Year	Cost	Comment
UAW Funerals	1963	$1520[a] $1580[b]	
	1965	$1560[a] $1600[b]	All Workers Studied
National Funeral Directors Assoc.	1962	$ 763[b]	Excludes burial vaults, clothing, clergy fees, flowers
International Ladies Garment Workers Union	1963	$ 924[b]	Excludes cemetery plots, headstones, and outside city transportation
Jessica Mitford	1960	$1160 $1450[b]	Higher estimate includes extras
Ruth Harmer	1960	$1100[b]	Adult funerals
	1962	$1400[b]	
	1963	$1546[c]	Counting the trimmings
Magrisso & Rubin	1961	$ 800[c]	Standard funeral
Senators Hart, Dodd, and T. Kennedy	1963	$ 988[b]	Based on U. S. Dept. of Commerce figures

[a]Median
[b]Average
[c]Other or not specified.

A Comparison of Funeral Costs

It is difficult to make meaningful comparisons between the funeral cost experience of Detroit-based auto worker survivors and similar experience of other groups of survivors. In addition to the nature of their employment, the age distribution and family characteristics of the deceased groups differ. The latter variations would have to be controlled before generalizations could be made. In addition, the years studied differ and few of the studies on funeral costs have agreed on the definition and measurement of included costs.

On the basis of the overall data, however, it appears that funeral costs for Detroit auto workers in this study (particularly in the 1963 group to which other data are most comparable) were somewhat higher than the average reported for other groups as summarized in Table 5-5. In fact, the *median* funeral cost of the survivors studied is as high as the reported estimate of a funeral with all the trimmings. Whether this is in any sense a result of the lump sum group insurance benefit which undertakers know auto workers to have can only be speculated upon.

The range of cost estimates is as varied as the estimators. Jessica Mitford suggests that the average cost for regular adult funerals in 1960 was at least $1160 or as high as $1450 if extras are included.[1] Ruth Mulvey Harmer estimated that the average cost of adult funerals in 1960 was $1100 and by mid-1962 was about $1400.[2] Magrisso and Rubin have estimated the going price of a standard funeral in 1961 to be about $800.[3]

A representative of the National Funeral Directors Association, a funeral industry trade association, testified (in a hearing of the Senate Sub-Committee on Antitrust and Monopoly) that according to NFDA studies, the national average funeral cost in 1962 was $763.[4] This estimate does not include the cost of burial vaults, clothing, fees for clergymen, and flower expenses. An average cost estimate which includes these items and is more directly comparable to this study was submitted in testimony to the same Sub-Committee by a representative of the International Ladies Garment Workers Union (ILGWU); who reported that the 1963 average funeral bill submitted to the ILGWU for payment on behalf of its members was $924.[5] This figure, however, excluded expenses for cemetery plots, headstones, and transportation outside the city. The highest estimate (by an executive of an organization of Chicago cemeteries) is reported by Harmer. He estimated that the cost of dying in 1963, counting the trimmings was $1546.[6]

The U.S. Department of Commerce estimated total personal expenditures for funeral and burial expenses in 1963 to be $1.8 billion.[7] The Department of Commerce estimate includes expenditures for indigent and infant funerals. It takes into account costs of funeral director services, caskets, crematories, monuments, opening and closing graves, and so on. Based on this figure, Senators Philip A. Hart (Chairman), Thomas J. Dodd, and Edward M. Kennedy estimated an average cost of $988 per funeral in 1963.[c]

---

[c]Senate subcommittee on Antitrust and Monopoly, *Antitrust Aspects of the Funeral Industry,* 1967. This report also cites figures reported in the 1963 Census of Business, showing $1298 million as total receipts in 1963 for all funeral homes and crematories. This figure averages to $716 per funeral in 1963. (p. 5) Senators Dirksen and Hruska cite this figure in their separate view published with the report, attacking the misstatements of fact in the Hart view. According to Senators Dirksen and Hruska, "The Hart view listed an estimated $1,793 million or an average of $988 per funeral of personal expenditures for funeral and burial expenses for 1963 whereas the U.S. Commerce actual figures for 1963 were $1,298 million or $723 on an average per funeral." (p. 55). It must be emphasized, however, that the reported $1,298 million figure represents the total annual 1963 *receipts*

The median 1963 auto worker cost, as noted in Table 5-2 was $1520, and the mean was $1580. The latter figures also include the above costs but, of course, exclude infant and indigent funeral expenses.[d] This compares with the above published estimates of mean funeral costs (covering 1960 to 1963) which range from $763 to $1546 both for 1963.

Comparing means and medians when the distributions are not fully known is not possible. However, based on the above published figures (summarized in Table 5-5), it is reasonable simply to conclude that mean funeral costs for the Detroit area auto workers in the study at least equaled $1546, the highest estimated funeral costs counting the trimmings (see report by Harmer above) and were well above the $988 national average expenditure for 1963 (see *Antitrust Aspects of the Funeral Industry*).

Auto worker funerals appear relatively expensive. However, as was cited above, the $988 figure is deflated by the inclusion of infant and indigent funerals. The auto worker funerals may also have been relatively costly because of the availability of insurance proceeds to the survivors. This cannot be tested with the present data.

Utilization Generally

After paying all the expenses associated with the worker's death and using the proceeds for various other expenses, the 1963 survivors replying reported median group insurance proceeds left of approximately $1750; less than half the $4080 reported by 1965 survivors as left at the time of their interview. At the other extreme, more than twice as many of the 1963 survivors reported having none of the group insurance proceeds left. Thirteen percent of the 1963 survivors and 33% of the 1965 survivors had $5000 or more remaining.

The above is an expected reflection of the different stage of adjustment and the greater benefits paid on average in 1965. Table 5-6 shows the percentage distribution of the insurance proceeds retained at the time of interview. It offers

for two major participants in the funeral industry; funeral homes and crematories. Obviously, they are not the *only* participants. This figure does not include 1963 receipts for cemeteries, manufacturers of grave markers, florists, clergymen, etc. The Department of Commerce $1,793 million figure (used by Senator Hart) on the other hand, represents *personal consumption expenditures* or the total amount spent in 1963 by individuals for funeral and burial expenses.

[d]Other published reports utilize the average or arithmetic mean (X) as a measure of central value. This report utilizes the median (md) which is considered less sensitive than the mean to distortions caused by extreme values. In symmetrical distributions the average is located at the center of symmetry. In nonsymmetrical distributions the average may vary from the distribution midpoint. The median, however, in *any* distribution is always such that one-half of the cases have higher values and the other half have lower values. The range reported for UAW member funerals ($40 to $4411) is nearly as wide as the national range. However, the number of cases (and the percent) at the extremes is much smaller. Thus the UAW mean would be less sensitive to extreme variation than national data.

Table 5-6

**Proceeds from Group Life Insurance
Retained at Time of Interview[a]
(% Distribution)**

Amount Retained	1963	1965
N =	340	395
None	27%	13%
Less than $1000	9	5
$1000-$1999	12	7
2000- 2999	7	9
3000- 3999	11	11
4000- 4999	10	13
5000- 5999	4	9
6000- 6999	5	13
7000- 7999	2	6
8000 +	2	5
No Answer	11	9
	100%	100%
Median	$1750	$4080

[a]Dependent survivors only; median
excludes no answer.

a large measure of support for the hypothesis offered in Chapter 2—that survivor benefits were adequate to meet immediate financial requirements related to the death of the worker.

After funeral expenses, which all but three respondents cited, the second most frequently mentioned use of insurance proceeds (1963 survivors), was ordinary living expenses, including rent, taxes, groceries, clothes, payments on houses, and so on. The use category—Put in bank; saved it; invested in stocks, bonds, mutual funds, credit union, real estate or own business—was the third in importance for the 1963 group. The above two categories—Consumption and

Table 5-7

**Most Frequently Reported Uses of
Life Insurance Proceeds[a]
(% Distribution)**

Uses	1963	1965
N =	340	395
1. Ordinary living expenses; rent, taxes, groceries, clothes, etc.	49%	35%
2. Put in bank, other savings, or investments	39	46
3. Paid off mortgage or buy house	21	16
4. Bought durable goods; home repairs, improvement, appliances, etc.	21	14
5. Doctor bills, other health expenses	15	7
6. Bought a car	11	6
7. Gave or loaned money to friends or relatives; paid daughter's hospital bills, used to support mother, etc.	9	6
8. Education or savings for future education of widow or children	4	4

[a]Dependent survivors only; excludes use on worker's funeral. More than one use was frequently reported by survivors; therefore, figures do not add to 100%.

Saving—changed relative positions in the 1965 group, again consistent with the survivor's state of adjustment.

Table 5-7 ranks the most frequently mentioned uses of life insurance proceeds, other than expenses directly associated with worker's death, by relative frequency. Items 1, 5, and 7 represent current consumption (direct or indirect); 2, 3, and 8 represent investment (tangible or intangible); 4 and 6 represent purchase of consumer durable goods.

Table 5-8 summarizes the uses of group insurance proceeds by type of use. Both tables reveal a major difference between the survivors for the two years

Table 5-8

Use of Group Insurance Proceeds[a]
(% Distribution)

	1963	1965
N =	340	395
Current Consumption	74%	48%
Consumer Durable Goods	32	21
Investment	65	66

[a]Includes multiple uses, so does not add to 100%.

studied. Though the percentage reporting investment uses is roughly constant for the two groups, less than half of the 1965 survivors report using the group insurance proceeds for current consumption as compared to nearly three-fourths of the 1963 group. Moreover, while the number investing is roughly constant, the amount of money reported as still invested by the 1965 group is considerably higher than for the 1963 survivors.

Independent of the use of group insurance proceeds, dependent beneficiaries were asked about their retention and purchase of life insurance. For both years studied, 83% of the dependent family units reported that they had had life insurance on the widow and/or other dependents at the time of the worker's death. Of these, 52% had insurance on the widow only, while 43% covered the children as well. Ninety-two percent reported that all of this insurance was retained at the time of the interview. A smaller percentage (88%) of the 1963 survivors had retained all of their insurance coverage.[e]

It is perhaps indicative of the survivors' attitude toward death and insurance that 25% of all dependent units reported the purchase of additional life insurance since the worker's death, a greater percentage than those dropping coverage. Fifty-five percent of this new insurance was on the widow only.

[e]For the U.S. in 1965, about two out of three wives had some form of life insurance coverage. In 1960, nearly three out of five female heads of household were covered by private life insurance. *Life Insurance Fact Book*, 1967, pp. 8-9. Thus, the women studied, both as wives and widows, had a somewhat higher percent of coverage than was found in the entire United States adult female population. Amount of coverage of those studied is not known.

Personal Implications of the Breadwinner's Death

In the earliest planning of this study, a great deal of attention was to have been paid to the social and psychological as well as the economic consequences of the breadwinner's death upon his dependent survivors. It soon became apparent, however, that the task of collecting the necessary economic data (by questionnaire and other sources) was so formidable and time-consuming that scant resources remained for any detailed questioning of noneconomic factors. Yet, it seemed important to interview the survivors (at least briefly) on such matters as the impact of the death on the children and on plans for their education; the use of financial and family counseling services; and the social adjustment of the widow in terms of her group memberships and leisure time activities.

Any one of the above areas of investigation could perhaps support a full-scale study in itself and no claim is made to have fully covered any of them. The data to be presented in this chapter are nevertheless of interest and importance, both in their own right and as they help to place the economic impact of the wage earner's death in a broader context and thus improve understanding of the survivors' total adjustment.

Demographic Considerations

Data in this chapter cover only the widows of the deceased auto workers and their dependent children, if any. The personal implications of the breadwinner's death are much less consequential to our study when the survivors are more distantly related or not dependent on the deceased breadwinner, and inclusion of the rare cases in which dependents but no widow survive (for example, dependent children only, dependent sister) would only complicate the analysis. The widows studied are by far the largest group defined to have been dependent survivors. They are a homogeneous group in that all of them lived in the same relationship to the worker.

The widows are also fairly homogeneous with respect to age. Approximately 70% of both the 1963 and 1965 groups were in their forties or fifties at the time of interview, and most of the others were 60 or more. Only about one widow in ten was under 40. At interview, median age of the widows was approximately 53, about 4 years younger than the deceased husband. As indicated in Chapter 3, exclusion of accidental death cases (relatively young) would leave an even more homogeneous group of surviving widows.

The widows do differ, however, on one important factor, as shown in Table 6-1. At the time of interview, slightly fewer than half had dependent children;

Table 6-1

Dependents of Widows
(% Distribution)

	1963	*1965*
N =	325	367
Units With:		
One or more children under age 9	4%	7%
Dependent children aged 9-20 only	42	41
No children but other dependents	4	6
No dependents, widow only	50	46
	100%	100%

the remainder did not. Exactly half of the 1963 group and almost half of the 1965 group were left alone without other dependents. A few, with no children or with grown children, were left with other dependents, usually a parent or other relative. Among those with children, it may be seen that few had any youngsters under nine years of age;[a] the overwhelming majority had only older children. As might be expected, the younger children are more likely to be found among the more recently widowed group.

In addition to the loss of the chief wage earner, the postdeath size of family did decline from the predeath level. In part, this is the natural result of dependents aging and leaving home. While it is felt that some of this movement may have been directly or indirectly related to the death of the chief wage earner, this hypothesis was not tested.

The attitudes, and in a few cases the behavior, of the widows toward remarriage was investigated in the interview. It is not surprising, of course, as reported in Table 6-2, that a much higher proportion of the 1963 group had remarried by the time of interview—8%, as compared with only 1% of the more recently bereaved—but otherwise, as shown in the two Total columns, the two groups have much the same attitudes. Close to two-thirds of both groups say they probably or definitely will not remarry.

Among the 1963 group, intentions to remarry seem rather strongly related to whether or not the widow has dependents in her care. Eleven percent of those widowed and left with dependents in 1963 had already remarried by time of interview and an additional 17% said they definitely or probably would remarry.

[a]In this chapter, children under the age of nine are considered for special analysis. Elsewhere, age 13 is a cutoff point utilized. Generalizations based on either age are not affected by substituting the alternative age as few children and fewer family units (27) are involved.

Table 6-2

**Remarriage Plans of Widows
(% Distribution)**

	1963			1965		
	Depen-dents	No Depen-dents	Total	Depen-dents	No Depen-dents	Total
N =	163	162	325	198	169	367
Already remarried	11%	5%	8%	1%	–%	1%
Definitely plan to remarry	1	1	1	1	3	2
Probably will remarry	16	5	10	7	7	7
Probably will not	26	29	27	34	28	31
Definitely will not	31	43	37	30	47	38
Don't know	15	17	17	27	15	21
	100%	100%	100%	100%	100%	100%

Among those without dependents only 5% had remarried by time of interview and only 6% expressed any intention to do so. Of course, age of widow and the presence of dependents are closely related.

The relationship between remarriage plans and number of dependents is much less marked among the 1965 group of survivors although it may be observed that fully 75% of the unencumbered 1965 widows say they probably or definitely will not remarry. Those with dependents are no more likely to indicate positive intentions, but they are much more likely to express indecision. Thus, even within a year or so of their widowhood, those with dependents are much less likely to foreclose the idea of remarriage.

It was noted (not shown in table) that among the small group of widows who were left with children under nine, remarriage and plans to remarry are much more frequent. More than 20% of the 1963 widows with young children had remarried at time of interview, and a similar proportion expressed intentions to do so. Among the 1965 group with small children, 20% said they probably or definitely would remarry and another 44% answered "Don't know." Only about one-third answered negatively.

Sources of Financial Advice

For many of the widows interviewed, their husband's death must have posed awesome responsibilities in the acquisition and management of the various benefits to which they were entitled. No direct measures of the financial sophistication or acumen of the widows was obtained. It is known, however, that more than two-thirds of them did not finish high school. It is also known from responses to the question, "Who usually handled the money in your family before your husband's death?" that fewer than one-third of the widows said that they themselves did, although another one-third replied that they participated in the money management.

A variety of financial counseling services were presumably available (directly or indirectly) to the widows; their bank, an attorney, a union representative, the automobile company, the insurance man, and so on. Yet, as is shown in Table 6-3, almost four-fifths of the widows either consulted nobody or relied on the advice of a family member. Another 5% said the person they relied on most for advice about handling the family's financial matters was the mortician or undertaker.

Table 6-3

Primary Source of Postfatality Financial Advice (% Distribution)

	1963 Widows	*1965 Widows*	*All Widows*
N =	325	367	692
Self	38%	37%	37%
A family member, relative	43	40	42
Banker, bank employee	1	1	1
Auto company representative	–	1	*
Union representative	1	1	1
Clergyman	1	1	1
Mortician, undertaker	6	5	5
Attorney, lawyer	5	7	6
Insurance agent, company	1	*	1
Other: neighbor, friend	5	7	6
	100%**	100%	100%

*less than 0.6%
**may not add due to rounding

Almost two-thirds of the widows relied only on themselves or one other person to guide them in handling financial matters. When asked, "Was there anybody else whose financial advice you relied on at that time?" 64% answered, "No." Of those who did seek a second source of advice, almost half referred to another family member.

Further analysis of these data fails to show any evidence that the better educated widows relied more heavily on expert financial advice. They did, however, rely more often on themselves and less often on other family members. Only 35% of the widows who failed to complete high school relied on themselves, as compared with 41% of those who finished high school and 59% of the small number who attended college.[b]

The majority of the widows were apparently satisfied with the advice they received. Asked, "Where would you go today if you needed advice about financial matters?" 60% gave the same answer as before. More than one-fifth (22%), however, said if they had it to do over they would consult somebody else, and almost as many (18%) said they didn't know if they would talk to the same person or not. Interestingly, the most frequently mentioned source of advice among those who would do it differently today was not a family member or friend, but an attorney. Close to half (43%) of those who would seek a different financial adviser today said they would see a lawyer. The reasons for this reply were not given, but its implications are significant.

Effects on Social Activities

In the absence of empirical data, one could invent plausible but contradictory hypotheses about the effect of widowhood on the survivor's social activities. One might expect, for example, that her grief or her preoccupation with financial matters or with her dependent children would lead her to withdraw from groups and organizations she may formerly have been active in and to reduce her social and entertainment activities. Alternatively, one might argue that faced with the loss of her husband's companionship, and especially if she lacked family responsibilities, the widow would increase her social activities, become more active in groups or associations, and attempt to widen her circle of friends and acquaintances. Evidence from the present study strongly supports the first rather than the second hypothesis.

Forty-six percent of the 1963 widows, but only thirty-four percent of the 1965 widows, said that before their husband's death they belonged to one or more groups, clubs, or organizations.[c] The reason for the difference between the

---

[b]It is perhaps noteworthy also that none of these college-educated widows relied on the undertaker for financial advice.

[c]Twelve of the 325 (1963) widows and 11 of the 367 (1965) widows did not answer for themselves. But to avoid awkward exposition of the findings the data are presented as if the widow herself was in all cases the actual respondent.

two groups in this respect is not apparent, although it is the relatively smaller percentage of 1965 widows without children who lower the average for their group. Of the 1965 widows, those with children were approximately as likely to have been group members as the 1963 widows.

The above proportions are, in any case, close to the national average of 36 percent who answered affirmatively to a similar question.[1] The national survey, however, reported lower averages for blue-collar workers (32% for skilled workers and 23% for semiskilled) and for big city dwellers (32%), so perhaps these wives of auto workers are more likely to have been joiners than their social class or place of residence would indicate.

The types of organizations of which the widows were members were primarily religious or ethnic. Approximately two-thirds of all the joiners reported such membership. Next in popularity were social, hobby, or recreational groups, to which almost one-third of the joiners belonged. Almost one-fourth of the 1963 widows who belonged to a group prior to their husband's death, but only about one in seven of the 1965 widows, said they were members of some educational or cultural organization, including the PTA. (This is surprising, given the relatively higher percentage of 1965 widows with children). Smaller numbers mentioned civic or political groups, such as the League of Women Voters, and professional or work-related organizations including women's auxiliaries of local unions. Many widows, of course, belonged to more than one type of group.

Those widows who reported a group membership before their husband's death were asked, "Would you say you were a very active member of the group, a fair active member, or were you not very active in the group?" This question was then followed by: "And how about today—Are you very active in the group, fairly active, not active or do you no longer belong to it?" The results, with percentages based on only minority of widows (including those remarried) who had been members of a group are shown in Table 6-4. For both the 1963 widows and the 1965 widows they reveal a significant decline in group activity. Thirteen percent of the 1963 widows and eight percent of the 1965 widows who formerly belonged to a group no longer claim any membership, and the proportion who describe themselves as not active has greatly increased. There is a corresponding large decline in the proportion who say they are very active in the group.

Few of the widows—only 14% of the 1963 group and 9% of the 1965 group—say that they have joined any clubs or organizations since their husband's death.

Further evidence of a lower level of social activity among the women after their husband's death is apparent from the figures in Table 6-5. Toward the close of the interview, widows were asked, "We are interested in how certain of your activities may have changed since your husband died. For example, do you watch television more now, or less, or about the same as before?" The same question was then repeated concerning movie attendance, visiting friends, and inviting friends to visit you. It had been hypothesized that the widows would spend more time watching televison, but it seems that in total about as many

Table 6-4

Group Activities of Widows

	Widows Who Belonged to a Group, Club, or Organization (% Distribution)			
	1963 Widows		1965 Widows	
	Before Death	*After Death*	*Before Death*	*After Death*
N =	150		125	
Very active in group	65%	38%	45%	31%
Fairly active	26	19	38	29
Not active	9	30	17	32
No longer a member	–	13	–	8
	100%	100%	100%	100%

devote less time to this activity as devote more. Among the older widows, there is indeed a net increase in televiewing, as 33% say they watch more and only 28% say they watch less. But among the 1965 group the proportions are approximately reversed.

One possible explanation for the above is that widows with dependent children are much less likely to watch television than those without dependents—and the younger widows are more likely to have minor children. Perhaps a more important explanation suggested by Table 6-5, is that the social activities of the more recently widowed have not declined as much as those of the earlier group of widows. Television for the 1963 widows is now apparently serving as a partial replacement for the movie going, visiting, and other activities they formerly engaged in.

For each of the other three activities inquired about, a preponderance of both groups of widows say they are engaging in it less rather than more, and for each of the three activities the 1963 widows are considerably less active than the more recently bereaved. Thus, 43% of the 1963 group say they are going to the movies less often as compared with only 26% of the 1965 group; 39% of them visit friends less now, as compared with only 30% of the more recent group; and 44% invite friends in less often now as compared with only 32% of the 1965 widows.

One would perhaps have expected a reverse finding; a sharp decline in social

Table 6-5

**Change in Widow's Activities since
Husband's Death (% Distribution)**

	1963 widows	1965 widows
N =	325	367
Watch television:		
More	33%	25%
Less	28	33
About same or don't know	39	42
Go to the movies:		
More	7	5
Less	43	26
About same or don't know	50	69
Visit friends:		
More	21	25
Less	39	30
About same or don't know	40	45
Invite friends in to visit:		
More	14	16
Less	44	32
About same or don't know	42	52

activity in the year or so following the death, and then a gradual resumption of such acitivity. That this group of 1963 widows did not resume their former activities but rather continued their disengagement strongly confirms the fact that widows have many other problems besides financial ones. The relatively worse financial position of 1963 widows (at interview) and their relatively higher age are significant factors in explaining the above. An additional factor possibly explaining the above is the larger percentage of 1963 widows working at the time of interview.

Working widows in each of the two groups are much less likely to watch television. Employed widows in the 1963 group report lower movie attendance and less entertaining at home, but are as likely as the nonemployed to say they visit friends. Employed widows in the 1965 group do not differ from the nonemployed in their movie attendance, but as might be expected given their fuller schedule, are markedly less likely to visit friends and somewhat less likely to report entertaining at home. No additional evidence to enable the reader to explain the above behavior can be offered.

Effects on Children

There is scarcely need for survey evidence to document the obvious fact that the death of a father will profoundly affect the attitudes, behavior, and prospects of the dependent children he leaves behind. To derive general insights as to the extent of these effects on children, it seemed appropriate to include a few specific questions directed to those widows with minor children. Three areas of child activity were covered: how well the children were doing in school; how often the children visit in friends' homes or have friends visit them; and how often the children take part in group activities with other children. Ratings on each of the three were obtained from the mother at two points in time: retrospectively, before the father's death, and again as of time of interview. Table 6-6 shows relevant selected percentages regarding the above questions.

In all of these comparisons and for both groups of widows, it may be seen that more of the children are doing poorly in school and more of them are not participating in social activities since their father's death than before. The effect on the childrens' school work seems particularly striking: a doubling in the proportion of the 1963 group who are not doing well and more than a tripling among the more recently bereaved children. The proportion doing very well in school (not shown in the table) reveals a corresponding trend. Whereas 46% and 45% of the two groups of widows, respectively, said the children were doing very

Table 6-6

Children's Behavior before and after Father's Death (% Distribution)

| | Widows with children under 18 | | | |
| | 1963 Group | | 1965 Group | |
	Before Death	*At Interview*	*Before Death*	*At Interview*
N =	131		146	
Percent Who Say:				
Children doing not so well in school	5%	10%	6%	20%
Children visit friends or have them in only once a month or less	6	15	11	13
Children take part in group activities only once a month or less	28	38	25	33

well in school before the death, only 33% of the 1963 widows and only 26% of the 1965 group said they were doing very well at time of interview.

Two questions were also asked concerning the possible effect of the father's death on plans for sending the children to college. Among the 1963 group of widows, 58% told interviewers that before their husband's death there were plans to send one or more of the children on to college. Asked, "And how about now—Are there (still) plans to send them to college?", only 46% said that a child was actually attending college or that they still planned to send him. Of the 12% attrition, seven % joined the group who said they had no such plans and five % were added to the doubtful group who answered, "Maybe, I don't know." Among the 1965 group, on the other hand, there was no net change at all in plans. Both before the death and at time of interview, 55% of the widows said they had college plans for the children, 22% were doubtful, and 23% answered negatively.

A direct explanation of the above finding is not possible at present. Certainly the older widows, on the average, are closer to the point of actual decision about college and their current intentions may thus have been more realistic than those of the 1965 widows. In addition, as shown in Chapter 4, the financial impact of the death on the 1965 survivors was less extreme than for the 1963 group and the full effect may not yet have been felt.

In any case, the widows reported that financial reasons, rather than any other, accounted for the great majority of changes of plan. Of those who had planned to send children to college but now were doubtful or negative, 63% of the 1963 group and 64% of the 1965 group explained that they felt they no longer could afford the costs of college.

Sources of Advice About Children

It may be surmised that those widows with dependent children may also have felt the need for outside advice—professional or otherwise—in handling teenagers or younger children suddenly left fatherless. Toward the close of the interview, the interviewer said to such widows: "We all know that it's not often easy to raise a family, and that problems may come up which are difficult even for two parents to handle. In such cases, parents sometimes seek the help or advice of people outside the family." She then asked: "During the year or so before your husband's death, did you or your husband ever turn to anyone for help or advice about your children?" And finally: "And since his death, have you turned to anyone for help or advice about your children?" The findings are shown in Table 6-7.

It seems clear from the "Before Death" column that few auto workers or their wives turn outside the family for advice about raising their children during any twelve-month period. National or other figures with which these data may be compared have not been located. While some widows may have been reluctant to confess their need for outside help in these matters, thus lowering

Table 6-7

Outside Advice about Children
(% Distribution)

	1963 Widows		1965 Widows	
	Before Death	*Since Death*	*Before Death*	*Since Death*
N =	131		151	
Sought help or advice	8%	29%	9%	17%
Did not seek advice	92	71	91	83
	100%	100%	100%	100%

the proportions who answered Yes, there are two considerations which might even have led to exaggeration in these figures. Although the question referred to sources outside the family, the word family can be ambiguously interpreted as either outside the household or from people other than relatives. (This, however, applies both before and after the worker's death). Among the sources of advice actually mentioned were parents and other relatives, so that if these are subtracted, the proportion is even smaller. Furthermore, the question inquired about the year or so before your husband's death. In many cases, this would have been a period of declining health on the part of the father, a time when the mother might have especially needed help with her children's problems.

At any rate, it is plainly evident that outside help concerning children's problems was sought by much higher proportions of the widows after their husband's death. In the four to sixteen months which elapsed since the death in the 1965 group, 17% of the widows sought such help, virtually twice the number which had sought it during the year preceding the death. Among the 1963 group, which of course had a longer period over which to seek help, 29% acknowledged that they had done so.

The problems for which the parents had sought help before the husband's death were normally school-related. More than half of those who saw an outside adviser during that period were concerned about the child's problems in school. No special source of advice seemed to be preferred. Relatives, clergymen, family counselors, doctors, and school officials were all mentioned about equally. The majority of visits after the father's death, however, were not about school problems but reflected the loss of the father. About one-third of the widows who sought outside help had problems with the child's mental or emotional adjustment to the loss, and about one-fourth simply felt they needed help in raising the child without a father in the home. These two groups together accounted for the majority of consultations in this period. Again, no particular source of advice was mentioned by more than about one-third. Most frequently referred to were teachers or school officials, doctors, and relatives.

Respondents were asked to rate each source of help they mentioned as very helpful to you, fairly helpful, or no real help at all. Unfortunately, no source was mentioned often enough to provide enough cases for a stable estimate. If all the sources seen after the death are added together, it appears that the majority (55%) were rated as very helpful and only 11% were regarded as no real help at all. This finding indicates that the mere fact of consultation may have been helpful.

While the number of cases is far too small to lend any statistical significance to the findings, it is perhaps of interest to note that family counselors and social workers, a combined category, were not rated as particularly helpful. Thus, of the seven widows who consulted this type of adviser about the children after their husband's death, only two found them very helpful and two others said they were no real help at all. Of the five who consulted a family counselor or social worker in the year preceding their husband's death, only one said she was really helped and three said the visit or visits were no help at all. The reasons for these low ratings of professional counselors can only be speculative. Perhaps the widows expected relatively more from such advisers; perhaps their contact with them was only a brief one.

Finally, the widows were asked, "Did you ever at any (other) time seek help from a professional agency, like a marriage counselor or social welfare agency about some personal or family problem?" Only 5% of both groups of widows answered this question affirmatively, and four-fifths or more of these said it was before their husband's death rather than after. Combining both groups of widows, there are only 29 cases, but again the results are suggestive. In reply to how much help these professional counselors had been, fewer than half (13 cases) answered very helpful and almost one-fourth (7 cases) said no real help at all. Again, these data cannot be compared to any national figures. However, in evaluating the use of counseling services by the group studied, the predeath use indicates limited exposure to such services.

Appendixes

Appendix A
Variations in Survivor
Adjustment Patterns

In Chapter 4, the immediate and ongoing adjustment of dependent survivors was considered. In Chapter 5, the uses of the group insurance proceeds by the dependent survivors were summarized. In this appendix, the results of cross-tabulating immediate survivor adjustment expenses (and selected components, for example, total family indebtedness, medical expenses, and funeral costs) and uses of group life insurance proceeds with selected characteristics of the survivors, for example, age, income, family size, and so on, are reported.

As observed elsewhere in the text, caution must be used in generalizing from these findings particularly as many of the categories reported include few cases and the statistical significance of the findings was not tested. They are reported, however, for those interested in the underlying data as well as the social and economic relations involved in the adjustment processes.

Immediate Adjustment Expenses

The costs of the immediate survivor adjustments were analyzed in relation to selected social and economic characteristics in an effort to identify meaningful variations in behavior. Four items associated with adjustment costs: (1) total family indebtedness at the time of worker's death; (2) postdeath medical charges incident to worker's last illness or accident; (3) funeral costs; and (4) total immediate adjustment costs were specifically analyzed.

Total Family Indebtedness

For purposes of this analysis, total family indebtedness is the sum of the amounts reported by respondents to the questions regarding loans and personal obligations owed by the family prior to the worker's death.[a] Total family indebtedness was cross-tabulated with selected worker-survivor social and economic characteristics, including age, widow work status, and so on. Table A-1 summarizes these cross-tabulations which are discussed below.

Number of Surviving Dependents. Fifty-four percent of the surviving (widow-headed) families had indebtedness (excluding mortgages) rising out of the deceased worker's obligations. Of those that owed money, the typical amount owed in this category in both years was less than $1,000. In both years, where the widow was the only survivor there was typically no debt obligation outstanding. Debt position is also a function of worker's and survivor's ages.

As may be expected, as the size of the family increases, so also does the amount of the worker's personal obligations and the percentage experiencing

---

[a]In the text material, indebtedness was analyzed independently and was not included in immediate adjustment expenses. As debt is relatively small and fairly widely distributed, it is believed that the generalizations are not altered appreciably by using either adjustment concept.

such obligations. This is particularly true for the 1965 families where four or more dependents survive. Where a dependent does not survive, (Short Form) significantly less worker debt was reported by the group insurance beneficiaries. In part, this finding may be based on a nondependent survivor's limited knowledge of the decedent. Again, generalization cannot be made for the small number of dependent surviving units not headed by a widow.

Age of Worker. When personal indebtedness is analyzed in terms of worker's age at time of death, it is noted that where debts existed, workers in the age group 35-44 held relatively higher debts. The extent of personal obligations fall off dramatically in older age groups.

Religion of Worker. Because of the small numbers involved it is possible to comment on differential indebtedness only by comparing Catholics and all Prostestants; and all Protestants with the Baptists in the group. Relative to the worker's religious preference, more Protestants reported indebtedness than Catholics. Of those in debt, moreover, Protestants had somewhat higher debts as well. Comparing all Protestants with the Baptist component, fewer of the latter were without debts and typically the amount of their debts was higher than the former. No attempt was made to isolate the effect of intervening variables such as income, education, and race. As noted in the discussion of religious characteristics of workers and survivors in Chapter 3, a given religious preference may be associated with such variables and may also be reflective of other factors (for example, influx of Southern black and white workers to Detroit plants during the 1940's).

Other Worker-Survivor Noneconomic Characteristics. Though chronically ill widows were more likely to have debt, no significant differences may be reported when indebtedness was cross-tabulated with (1) widow's evaluation of her own health; and (2) worker education.

Widow's Work Status. The relation of widow's work status at time of death and family indebtedness is not a strong one. In part, this may be explained by the variety of reasons wives work. In general, however, working widows were left with more large debts than those who were not working at the time of worker's death.

Comparing widows' employment status at the time of the interview with indebtedness at the time of the worker's death reveals that such working widows, if in debt, had higher debts—perhaps the result of greater ability to obtain debt. On the other hand, the largest percentage of widows working at the time of interview were free of debts at the time of the worker's death.

Family Financial Resources. A comparison of total family financial resources and total family indebtedness for worker loans and obligations at the time of the worker's death reveals the following: as total family assets increase in size, so also does the number of families who were free of indebtedness, that is, the

Table A-1

Median Family Indebtedness at Time of Worker's Death and Selected Worker-Survivor Characteristics

Family Size[b]

		Widow Only	Widow Plus			
			One	*Two*	*Three*	*Four +*
1963	N =	162	67	45	25	25
	Median	$800	$500	$710	$830	$1070
	% with debt	42%	55%	82%	72%	65%
1965	N =	172	79	54	27	35
	Median	$800	$650	$700	$570	$$990
	% with debt	40%	61%	63%	66%	88%

Age of Worker[c]

		25-34	*35-44*	*45-54*	*55-65*	*65 +*
1963	N =	8	31	118	168	13
	Median	$1040	$780	$844	$780	$450
	% with debt	50%	71%	60%	46%	55%
1965	N -	18	43	110	210	6
	Median	$682	$625	$875	$650	$765
	% with debt	79%	66%	58%	46%	17%

Religion of Worker[c]

		Catholic	All Protestants	Protestants Only	
				Baptist	*Other*
1963	N =	126	197	79	118
	Median	$620	$880	$750	$950
	% with debt	45%	59%	71%	53%
1965	N =	140	232	95	137
	Median	$790	$730	$640	$790
	% with debt	45%	56%	50%	50%

Widow's Health[b]

		Chronic Illness	
		Yes	*No*
1963	N =	111	212
	Median	$750	$830
	% with debt	60%	52%
1965	N =	112	256
	Median	$770	$770
	% with debt	56%	53%

Table A-1 (continued)

Worker's Education[c]

		8th grade or less	Some high school	Completed high school	Some College	Don't Know
1963	N =	157	91	49	18	25
	Median	$900	$750	$750	$360	$500
	% with debt	51%	56%	59%	56%	68%
1965	N =	174	109	69	17	26
	Median	$680	$650	$1150	$450	$690
	% with debt	59%	53%	55%	53%	62%

Widow's Work Status at Time of Interview[b]

		Working		Not Working
		Full Time	Part Time	
1963	N =	108	59	158
	Median	$1050	$830	$690
	% with debt	53%	49%	59%
1965	N =	88	35	244
	Median	$1000	$920	$680
	% with debt	51%	57%	56%

Financial Resources at time of death[c]

		No Answer	None	< $2000	$2000 -3999	$4000 -5999	$6000 +
1963	N =	18	98	125	32	22	45
	Median	$500	$890	$770	$920	$390	$800
	% with debt	44%	70%	62%	44%	36%	27%
1965	N =	19	100	136	52	24	64
	Median	$750	$800	$500	$500	$750	$2000
	% with debt	22%	69%	60%	40%	50%	31%

Amount of Other Life Insurance[c]

		None and No Answer	< $2000	$2000 -3999	$4000 -5999	$6000 +
1963	N =	93	152	59	18	18
	Median	$700	$810	$790	$1680	$750
	% with debt	45%	56%	61%	61%	72%
1965	N =	82	123	103	43	44
	Median	$800	$460	$710	$830	$750
	% with debt	43%	54%	56%	56%	64%

Table A-1 (continued)

Worker Skill Category[c]

		I	II	III
	N =	122	120	98
1963	Median	$870	$850	$620
	% with debt	57%	57%	51%
	N =	190	95	110
1965	Median	$650	$860	$710
	% with debt	54%	59%	47%

[a]Omits cases with no answer or with no indebtedness (except as otherwise indicated). Excludes home mortgage debt. Data for deaths involving all survivors:

	Nondependent Survivors		Dependent Survivors	
	1963	1965	1963	1965
Median debt	$640	$500	$790	$730
% with debt	29%	41%	54%	52%

[b]Widow-headed dependent surviving units only. For such units:

	1963	1965
N =	325	367
Median debt	$790	$740
% with debt	54%	54%

[c]Dependent survivors:

	1963	1965
N =	340	395

higher the resources the less the debts. The financial resources of the 1965 group were somewhat greater than those of the 1963 survivors.

Amount of Other Insurance. Almost all of the workers, 76% in 1963 and 83% in 1965, had some form of other benefit in addition to negotiated group life insurance and Social Security. Not all provided a cash yield, however. There were more respondents free of debts in both years among those in the group that reported having had no other form of insurance. It may be hypothesized that with less debt, there is less demand for additional insurance. This hypothesis was not tested.

Worker Skill. For those with dependent survivors, the worker in the highest skill category (III) left fewer debts in both years. The amount of debt where debts were present, however, does not seem to be related to the degree of worker skill.

Total Medical Expenses

As indicated in Chapter 4, about 36% of the 1963 group and 33% of the 1965 group had no postdeath medical charges to pay out-of-pocket incident to the worker's death. For those that had such bills, the typical amount due for both years was less than $100. As the number of survivors with significant medical charges is small, no tables are provided.

Age of Worker. For those with medical expenses, the larger amounts (as expected) were typically experienced by workers 45 years old and over. In all cases, median amounts for those with such expenses were less than $100.

Religion of Worker. Where comparing medical expenses and worker religion, it is noted that a higher percentage of Baptists were free of this expense in 1963 than Catholics and other Protestants. This difference, however, may not be observed with the 1965 survivors, and its rationale can only be speculative. Again, median medical expense for those with such expense was under $100. As stated previously, religion may be a proxy for such variables as race, income, and education. This was not tested, however.

Other Social Characteristics. No significant relationships were found between medical expenses and the other characteristics examined. About 3% of the 1963 cases and 7% of the 1965 cases belonged to the closed panel prepaid group practice Community Health Association.[b] The balance, less 7 cases in all who did not know, were covered by Blue Cross-Blue Shield service contracts.

The number of observations are clearly too small to permit extensive generalization. However, for the group studied, Blue Cross-Blue Shield subscribers were more likely to have out-of-pocket medical expenses payable after their death. Blue Cross subscribers included relatively more cases where the amount of charges payable approached cost extremes.

Survivors retained approximately the same degree of membership in CHA as did the deceased breadwinners.

Economic Characteristics. A higher than average (for the group as a whole) percentage of survivors with no financial resources at the time of the worker's death paid out-of-pocket medical expenses in both years. Still, with only two small subgroups in exception, median medical expenses were less than $100.

---

[b]In March 1965, a representative date for which figures are available for plants in which dual choice exists, 7% of Chrysler employees; 4% (Ford); and 3% (G.M.) belonged to CHA.

Relating skill categories to medical expenses, a higher percentage of the survivors of Category I workers (1963) reported no outstanding medical expenses. In 1965, this situation was reversed. No hypotheses can be offered to explain this difference between these subsamples. Without exception, the median medical outlays were again under $100.

1965 survivors had slightly more life insurance benefits from other than group life insurance sources than 1963 survivors. No significant relationship between such insurance and medical expenses payable after the worker's death was observed. Apparently, such coverage did not induce the incurring of (possibly optional) medical costs.

Thus, it appears that there is no clearly definable relationship between postdeath out-of-pocket medical charges and worker-survivor economic variables. This may be due to payment of medical charges prior to death or to absence of a strong relation between the small remaining medical charges and income for the covered workers.

Funeral Costs

The following worker-survivor demographic characteristics have been cross-tabulated with funeral costs:

1. For workers—age at time of death; country of birth; religious preference; and education.
2. For widows—age at time of interview; country of birth; religious preference; number of surviving dependents; and condition of health.

Since these variables, except widow's health are correlated for worker and widow, similar patterns with respect to funeral cost may be expected. In addition, some of the variables (for example, age and widow's health) are also correlated and these must be analyzed together to eliminate intervening effects.

In examining the first set of variables above, insights into the influence the deceased could exercise over his own funeral were sought. In addition, since the widow generally made (or implicitly approved) the actual burial decisions, information on these decisions relative to selected characteristics is presented.

Briefly summarizing the basic data and the highlights of the tables:

1. Generally speaking, for workers leaving dependent survivors, the older the worker, the more costly the funeral. The greatest range of funeral expense was experienced with respect to workers in the predominant age group (age 55-64) at time of death (not shown in the table).
2. Considering funeral expenses by the widow's age, the most costly funerals in 1963, (costing $2000 or more) were typically purchased by surviving widows who were within the age range 45-54. The 1965 experience demonstrated an even more pronounced tendency for younger widows to spend less for

Table A-2

Median Funeral Costs[a]
Selected Worker Demographic
Characteristics

Age		35-44	45-54	55-64	65 +
Nondep.					
1963	N =	7	12	35	8
	Median	$1640	$1750	$1520	$1500
1965	N =	8	19	25	2
	Median	$2000	$1540	$1520	$1500
Dep.					
1963	N =	31	118	168	13
	Median	$1360	$1460	$1580	$1390
1965	N =	43	110	210	6
	Median	$1450	$1590	$1570	$2000

Country of Birth			U.S.A.	Canada	Other
Nondep.					
1963	N =		58	3	8
	Median		$1680	$1250	$1380
1965	N =		61	3	5
	Median		$1570	$1750	$1580
Dep.					
1963	N =		281	12	47
	Median		$1470	$1420	$1760
1965	N =		343	6	46
	Median		$1530	$1770	$1890

Religious Preference		Catholic	All Protestants	Protestant Only	
				Baptist	*Other*
Nondep.					
1963	N =	33	32	12	20
	Median	$1730	$1500	$1490	$1500
1965	N =	21	44	18	26
	Median	$1660	$1520	$1590	$1480

Table A-2 (continued)

Religious Preference		Catholic		All Protestants	Protestant Only Baptist	Protestant Only Other
Dep.						
1963	N =	126		197	79	118
	Median	$1610		$1450	$1390	$1470
1965	N -	140		232	95	137
	Median	$1760		$1440	$1350	$1540

Education		8th Grade or less	Some high school	Completed high school	Some College	Don't Know
Nondep.						
1963	N =	31	17	8	3	10
	Median	$1600	$1610	$1500	$1760	$1640
1965	N -	28	18	16	2	5
	Median	$1550	$1590	$1630	$1500	$1410
Dep.						
1963	N =	157	91	49	18	25
	Median	$1490	$1590	$1440	$1640	$1320
1965	N -	174	109	69	17	26
	Median	$1530	$1520	$1640	$1630	$1670

[a]Median funeral costs for all workers:

			1963	1965
Nondependent Survivors (Nondep.)	N =		69	69
	Median		$1620	$1570
Dependent Survivors (Dep.)	N =		340	395
	Median		$1490	$1550

Table A-3

Median Funeral Costs
Selected Widow Demographic
Characteristics[a]

Age at Interview[b]		25-34	35-44	45-54	55-64	65 +
1963	N =	7	2	124	121	26
	Median	$1790	$1390	$1500	$1600	$1520
1965	N =	19	54	149	120	19
	Median	$1340	$1460	$1650	$1580	$1650

Country of Birth				U.S.A.	Canada	Other
1963	N =			289	17	19
	Median			$1490	$1460	$1846
1965	N =			320	7	40
	Median			$1560	$1880	$1740

Religious Preference		Catholic	All Protestants	Protestant Only — Baptist	Protestant Only — Other
1963	N =	121	196	86	110
	Median	$1620	$1430	$1370	$1490
1965	N =	133	222	89	133
	Median	$1800	$1440	$1370	$1500

Number of Surviving Dependents		Widow Only	Widow plus — One	Two	Three	Four +
1963	N =	162	67	45	25	26
	Median	$1540	$1540	$1540	$1360	$1390
1965	N =	172	79	54	27	35
	Median	$1660	$1680	$1430	$1450	$1360

Chronic Illness					Yes	No
1963	N =				111	212
	Median				$1560	$1490
1965	N =				112	256
	Median				$1600	$1570

[a]Excludes families where widow didn't survive
    1963 (N − 325) Median − $1500
    1965 (N − 367) Median − $1580

[b]Widows averaged 4-5 years younger than husbands.

funerals while older widows seemed to spend the higher amounts. Again, this is not surprising, since younger widows generally received lesser amounts of insurance and had more numerous and younger dependents to support.

3. In general, the greater the number of dependents, the less reported as spent on funerals. In 1965 the group which experienced the highest funeral costs were the ones in which a widow and one other dependent survived. This is not the case in the 1963 study year, however, where costs declined where three or more dependents survived. No hypotheses are offered to explain this phenomenon. Among dependent survivors, in cases where a widow was among the survivors, the funeral costs tended to be higher.

   The highest median funeral expenses, however, were experienced in those cases where the beneficiaries had not been dependents of the worker. This is not unreasonable, since most such beneficiaries were closely related to the deceased and had independent sources of income.

4. Considering the surviving widow's health state and total funeral costs, one finds that the median funeral cost in both years was somewhat higher for widows who reported that they had a chronic illness or long-standing condition which requires regular treatment or care. . . The medians are: 1963—$1560 (chronic illness); $1490 (other); and 1965—$1600 (chronic illness); $1570 (other). The relation of age of widow and chronic illness probably explains much of this difference in that older widows (many with reported chronic illness) had relatively fewer independent children.

5. Variations in total funeral costs are also apparent when the variables of the worker's and widow's religious preferences are considered. Of the 856 responses reporting worker's religious preferences 320 or 37% were reported as Catholic. In both study years the median total funeral costs were significantly higher for Catholics than for Protestant workers. The medians (all survivors) are: 1963—$1640 and $1460; 1965—$1750 and $1450. (This variation is even more markedly observable among widows who express a Catholic religious preference.)

   The relation of Total Immediate Adjustment Expenses (funeral costs plus prefatality debts, and so on) and religion is the reverse and is discussed in the next section. It is not clear whether income or race or education, or a combination may be the intervening variables explaining this difference.

   Variations within Protestant denominations, when sufficient cases are available to allow for comparisons, are apparent but less consistent than the above. Where all Protestant denominations are considered, Baptist is the only denomination represented in a sufficient number of cases to allow for comparison with other Protestants. Omitting nondependent survivor cases, Baptists characteristically spent less on funerals than Other Protestants. Race or income variations may explain this difference, but these variables have not been analyzed.

6. For workers leaving dependent survivors, funeral costs were less variable the greater the worker's education (not shown). Thus, in 1963, for example, for those worker's with an eighth grade education or less, costs ranged from $500

Table A-4

Median Funeral Costs[a]
Selected Worker Financial Characteristics

Skill Category				I	II	III
Nondep.						
1963	N =			32	26	11
	Median			$1640	$1460	$1790
1965	N =			47		
	Median			$1580	$1500	$1670
Dep.						
1963	N =			122	120	98
	Median			$1500	$1420	$1600
1965	N =			190	95	110
	Median			$1500	$1520	$1710

Amount Other Life Insurance[b]		*None*[d]	$< 2000	*$2000- 3999*	*$4000- 5999*	*$6000 +*
1963	N =	93	152	59	18	18
	Median	$1610	$1470	$1420	$1590	$1700
1965	N =	82	123	103	43	44
	Median	$1610	$1560	$1470	$1630	$1650

Financial Resources at Death[c]			$< 2000	*$2000- 3999*	*$4000- 5999*	*$6000 +*
1963	N =		125	32	22	45
	Median		$1470	$1540	$1770	$1500
1965	N =		136	52	24	64
	Median		$1530	$1540	$1640	$1680

[a]For median for all workers, see note 1, Table A-2; unless otherwise indicated, data refer to workers leaving dependent survivors.

[b]Excludes negotiated group insurance.

[c]Savings plus equity in home; less debts.

[d]Includes no answer.

to over $3000. For those with some college education, all funeral costs fell within a $1000 to $3000 range. The median funeral cost for workers with some college education (1963 deaths) was $1640 as against $1490 for those with an eighth grade (or less) education. The relatively small number of survivors with some college education particularly limits the statistical significance of this finding.

7. Analysis of funeral costs by country of birth reveals that such costs for workers leaving dependent survivors are, on the average, somewhat higher for those born outside the United States. Again, the small number of such cases limits the significance of this finding.

In addition to the above demographic cross-tabulations, total funeral costs were cross-tabulated with selected economic measures. The cross-tabulated variables include:

1. For the worker—the worker's occupational skill;[c] the amount of privately arranged life insurance the worker had in force prior to death; and family financial resources prior to death.[d]

2. For the widow—the widow's employment status before worker's death; the widow's employment status at the time of the interview; and the presence or absence of a regular family monthly income from any source at the time of the interviews.

In all cases, as expected, the families that enjoyed greater direct or potential financial resources spent more on worker funerals. The direction of cause,

---

[c]Worker occupational skills were grouped into three categories. Category I was identified as unskilled; Category II, semiskilled; and Category III, skilled. It was apparent from the results of the pretest that respondents were unable to reply to questions about worker occupations in a manner which would allow groupings by degree of skill. Therefore, questions about worker occupations were excluded from the basic interview schedule. The above categories were derived from the face value of worker group life insurance contracts. The face value of these contracts are directly related to hourly rates of pay, which generally reflect skill differences, but also reflect other factors, for example, difficult work conditions. The categories are based on the following life insurance amounts.

	1963	1965
Category I	Under $6,500	Under $7,000
Category II	$6,500 to $7,000	$7,000 to $7,500
Category III	Over $7,000	Over $7,500

The 1965 categories were adjusted upward to take into account improvements made in the group life insurance program negotiated in 1964 by the UAW and Big Three manufacturers. The group life insurance amount represents an approximation of the worker's annual income on the job. Thus, for most widows its receipt represents more than a year's income, since taxes and work-related costs are not deducted.

[d]Family financial resources before worker's death are responses to questionnaire question numbers 55 and 58. Question 55 takes into account the value of the worker's home at the time of his death. Question 58 takes into account (1) cash savings in any form; (2) investment securities in any form; (3) real property, other than home, and (4) interest in a business—at the time of the worker's death.

Table A-5

Median Funeral Costs
Selected Widow Financial Characteristics[a]

Employment Status Prior to Worker Death	Working		Not Working
	Full Time	Part Time	
1963 N =	71	34	220
Median	$1380	$1090	$1490
1965 N =	82	22	263
Median	$1570	$1030	$1545

Employment Status at Interview	Yes		No
	Full Time	Part Time	
1963 N =	108	59	158
Median	$1620	$1240	$1490
1965 N =	88	35	244
Median	$1610	$1180	$1530

Presence of Regular Monthly Income	Yes[b]		No
	With Transition	Without Transition	
1963 N =		317	23
Median		$1500	$1530
1965 N =	345	39	11
Median	$1570	$1490	$1440

[a]Excludes dependent units not headed by widow at interview. See Table A-6, note 1, for median funeral costs for this group.

[b]Transition benefit not available for 1963; monthly income sources include Social Security, monthly payment of insurance, transition benefit, etc.

Table A-6

Median Funeral Costs
Selected Widow
Characteristics

Age at Interview		25-34	35-44	45-54	55-64	65 +
1963	N =	7	2	124	121	26
	Median	$1790	$1390	$1500	$1600	$1520
1965	N =	19	54	149	120	19
	Median	$1340	$1460	$1650	$1580	$1650

Country of Birth				U.S.A.	Canada	Other
1963	N =			289	17	19
	Median			$1490	$1460	$1846
1965	N =			320	7	40
	Median			$1560	$1880	$1740

			All	Protestant Only	
Religious Preference		Catholic	Protestants	Baptist	Other
1963	N =	121	196	86	110
	Median	$1620	$1430	$1370	$1490
1965	N =	133	222	89	133
	Median	$1800	$1440	$1370	$1500

Number of Surviving	Widow	Widow plus			
Dependents	Only	One	Two	Three	Four +
1963	N =	162	67	45	25	26
	Median	$1540	$1540	$1540	$1360	$1390
1965	N =	172	79	54	27	35
	Median	$1660	$1680	$1430	$1450	$1360

Chronic Illness					Yes	No
1963	N =				111	212
	Median				$1560	$1490
1965	N =				112	256
	Median				$1600	$1570

Table A-7

Median Immediate Adjustment Expenditures Selected Worker Characteristics[a]

Size of Family[b]

	Widow Only	Widow Plus			
		One	Two	Three	Four +
1963					
N =	162	67	45	25	26
Median	$2000	$1680	$2910	$2080	$2350
%over $4000	7%	11%	25%	4%	8%
1965					
N =	172	79	54	27	35
Median	$2290	$2170	$2170	$1880	$2780
% over $4000	8%	8%	6%	8%	17%

Worker's Age[c]

		35-44	45-54	55-64	65 +
1963					
N =		31	118	168	13
Median		$1810	$2240	$2100	$1850
% over $4000		6%	13%	10%	8%
1965					
N =		43	110	210	6
Median		$2100	$2270	$2210	$2510
% over $4000		9%	11%	7%	—

Worker's Religion

	Catholic	All Protestant	Protestant Only	
			Baptist	Other
1963				
N =	126	197	79	118
Median	$1920	$2230	$2261	$2140
% over $4000	10%	10%	7%	11%
1965				
N =	140	232	95	137
Median	$2410	$2000	$2000	$2050
% over $4000	9%	8%	6%	9%

Table A-7 (continued)

Education of Workers[c]

	8th grade or less	Some high school	Completed high school	Some college	Don't know
1963					
N =	157	91	49	18	25
Median	$2050	$2050	$2430	$2000	$2000
% over $4000	10%	8%	12%	11%	8%
1965					
N =	174	109	69	17	26
Median	$2000	$2210	$2480	$2260	$2640
% over $4000	8%	7%	14%	6%	12%

[a]Omits no answer. Funeral expense, debt, estate fees, etc. Differs from concept reported in Chapter 4 in that debt is included in variable.

[b]Surviving family units headed by widow; (see note 2, Table A-1).

[c]Dependent Survivors.

Note: Median post-death expenses:

All Dependent Survivors		Widow-Headed Survivor Units	
1963	*1965*	*1963*	*1965*
$2100	$2200	$2090	$2280

however, is not always clear. For some variables, for example, widow employment status at interview, funeral expenditure may be determining the widow's work choice. The relationship between financial resources and expenditures on funerals is most visible for the variables: family financial resources prior to death, worker occupational skills, and privately arranged life insurance in force.

The small number of cases in many of the important categories and the presence of intervening variables preclude firm generalization, particularly in the case of monthly income recipients versus others in the survivor sample.

Total Immediate Adjustment Expenses

In this section, a summary of cross-tabulations of total immediate adjustment expenses and selected social and economic survivor characteristics is presented. Table A-7 summarizes data on immediate adjustment expenses for the variables specified. Again, the small number of cases in many categories significantly restricts generalizations that may be made from the data presented.

Number of Surviving Dependents. For the widow-headed survivor families, in units where a widow only survives, as opposed to a widow plus one or more dependents, the immediate adjustment expenses tend to be slightly less.

Age of Workers. The families of middle aged workers, 45-54, tended in both years to have slightly higher overall immediate adjustment expenses. As expected, this is also true for the middle-age groups for widows.

Religion of Workers. The survivors of Catholic workers in 1963 experienced lower immediate adjustment expenses than those with other religious preference. This experience was reversed for the 1965 group. This contrasts with amount spent on funerals and may result from the lower average debt of Catholics. Widow religious preference data parallel worker religious preference experience.

Education of Workers. Immediate adjustment expenses show very little variation by level of education achieved. In 1965, however, the data suggest, although it is not considered statistically significant, the more advanced the worker's education, the higher the immediate adjustment expense.

Other Uses of Group Life Insurance Proceeds

Certain uses of group life insurance proceeds reported in Chapter 5 were grouped and further analyzed to identify the characteristics of the survivors who report them. The specific uses considered are (1) savings or investments; (2) pay off mortgage or buy house; (3) purchase household items; and (4) buy a car.

Selected Worker–Survivor Characteristics

When younger widows, 44 years of age or less, had group insurance proceeds beyond that necessary for immediate needs, they most frequently reported the related uses savings or investments, and pay off mortgage or buy house, in that order. Widows with larger families, regardless of age, also reported the same order of uses.

Tables A-8 and A-9 relate the age of the widow at the time of the interviews and number of worker dependents at the time of the worker's death and the four selected uses for both study years. Younger widows reported the uses tabulated relatively less frequently than older widows (not shown in the tables).

The four selected uses were also cross tabulated with (1) worker's education; (2) worker's country of birth; (3) worker's religious preference; (4) widow's religious preference; and (5) widow's country of birth. As might have been

Table A-8

**Selected Uses of Group Insurance
Proceeds and Median Age[a]**

	Saving or Investment	Pay Off Mortgage	Purchase Household Items	Buy a Car
1963				
N =	126	95	69	38
Median Age	55	52	53	50
% of Total	37%	28%	20%	11%
1965				
N =	171	88	53	25
Median Age	53	50	50	48
% of Total	43%	22%	13%	6%

[a]Dependent survivors only;–total
1963 = 340; 1965 = 395.

expected, however, no significant differences with respect to these uses were obtained when these worker-survivor characteristics were considered.

Selected Family Financial Characteristics

The four selected uses of worker's group life insurance proceeds were also analyzed in terms of (1) worker's skill category; (2) widow's employment status at time of worker's death; (3) widow's employment status at time of interview; (4) family financial resources at time of worker's death; (5) amount of other life insurance proceeds, privately arranged, available to the survivors; (6) widow's self reported condition of health; and (7) widow's country of birth.

Tables A-10-A-16 summarize these data. Here, the different stages of adjustment regularly differentiate the responses for the 1963 and 1965 groups. Most of the widows interviewed were not reported as employed outside the home either at the time of the worker's death or at the time of the interviews.

Table A-9

**Selected Uses of Group Insurance Proceeds
and Number of Dependents[a]
(% Distribution)**

Dependents	Saving or Investment		Pay Off Mortgage		Purchase Household Items		Buy a Car	
	% N[b]	% U[c]	% N	% U	% N	% U	% N	% U
1963								
Widow only	43%	55%	26%	44%	19%	43%	7%	29%
Widow Plus:								
one	39	21	22	16	15	14	18	32
two	27	10	31	15	27	17	13	16
three	36	7	52	14	28	10	24	16
four +	38	8	42	12	38	14	12	8
	–	100**	–	100**	–	100**	–	100**
1965								
Widow Only	53	53	17	34	9	30	3	24
Widow Plus:								
one	43	20	27	24	19	28	4	12
two	43	13	24	15	17	17	15	32
three	30	5	48	15	26	13	19	20
four +	43	8	31	13	17	11	9	12
	–	100**	–	100**	–	100**	–	100

[a]Long Form excluding surviving units not headed by a widow. N = 325 widows (1963) and 367 widows (1965).

[b]% N is percentage of widows with stated dependent status, reporting use. As more than one use may be reported, % does not add to 100%.

[c]% U is percentage of use reported by widows with stated dependent status.
**rounding error.

The proportion of those who responded savings or investments as a use, however, was somewhat higher for those who were working during either or both of these periods. The spread of responses for the other selected uses was relatively consistent throughout.

As expected, when family financial resources at the time of the worker's death was used as a variable, the greater the amount of such resources, the greater the proportion of responses indicating savings or investments as a use of group life insurance proceeds. This generalization is equally applicable to 1963 and 1965 survivors; again qualified by their different stages of adjustment.

Table A-10

Most Frequently Reported Survivor Uses of Group Life Insurance Proceeds by Worker Skill Classification[a] (% Distribution)

Most Frequently Reported Uses	*No. of Times Reported*	Skill Classification		
		Category I	*Category II*	*Category III*
1963				
N =		122	120	98
Savings or investments	133	41%	30%	48%
Pay off mortgage or buy house	98	30	31	26
Purchase household items	71	24	23	15
Buy a car	39	11	13	11
1965				
N =		190	95	100
Savings or investments	183	42%	56%	46%
Pay off mortgage or buy house	94	24	23	25
Purchase household items	56	17	14	10
Buy a car	25	9	3	5

[a]Dependent Survivors; as multiple uses were reported, data do not add to 100%.

Survivors who reported no financial resources at the time of the worker's death more frequently reported using insurance proceeds to pay off mortgage or buy a house than those who had such resources. Unlike the 1963 group, among the 1965 survivors a much greater proportion of those who had no prefatality financial resources reported purchase of a car as an insurance use than those who had such resources. Generally, the greater the amount of financial resources at the time of the worker's death, the less frequently reported is the use to buy a car. This may be because the existing automobile was newer, but this cannot be substantiated.

Table A-11

**Most Frequently Reported Survivor
Uses of Group Life Insurance Proceeds
by Widows' Work Status at Time of
Worker's Death[a] (% Distribution)**

Most Frequently Reported Uses	No. of Times Reported	Widow's Working		
		Full Time	Part Time	No.
1963				
N =		71	34	220
Savings or investments	126	51%	26%	37%
Pay off mortgage or buy house	95	28	29	30
Purchase household items	69	15	21	23
Buy a car	38	10	9	13
1965				
N =		82	22	263
Savings or investments	171	55%	36%	45%
Pay off mortgage or buy house	88	27	23	23
Purchase household items	53	16	5	15
Buy a car	25	6	5	7

[a]Excludes surviving dependent family units not headed by widows.

When worker skill categories are taken as a variable, dependent survivors oɪ the most and least skilled workers (skill categories I and III) showed a generally similar pattern of group life insurance use. Survivors of workers in the intermediate skill category (II) reported relatively less savings or investments in 1963 and relatively more in 1965. In considering this variable, the relation of skill category to amount of group life insurance (see footnote c, this appendix) should be noted.

Table A-12

Most Frequently Reported Survivor Uses of Group Life Insurance Proceeds by Widow's Work Status at Time of Interview[a] (% Distribution)

Most Frequently Reported Uses	No. of Times Reported	Widow's Working		
		Full Time	Part Time	No.
1963				
N =		108	59	159
Savings or investments	126	48%	37%	33%
Pay off mortgage or buy house	95	27	31	30
Purchase household items	69	15	36	20
Buy a car	38	10	15	11
1965				
N =		88	35	244
Savings or investments	171	53%	40%	45%
Pay off mortgage or buy house	88	24	26	24
Purchase household items	53	11	17	15
Buy a car	25	6	3	8

[a]See note a, Table A-11

Table A-13

**Most Frequently Reported Survivor
Uses of Negotiated Life Insurance
Proceeds by Total Family Financial
Resources at Time of Worker's Death[a]
(% Distribution)**

Most Frequently Reported Uses	No. of Times Reported	No Financial Resources	$0001- 1999	$2000- 9999	$10,000 +
1963					
N =		98	125	72	27
Savings or investments	133	24%	38%	51%	63%
Pay off mortgage or buy house	98	36	31	19	15
Purchase household items	71	22	27	15	4
Buy a car	39	14	14	6	4
1965					
N =		100	136	100	40
Savings or investments	183	30%	44%	50%	80%
Pay off mortgage or buy house	94	33	24	22	13
Purchase household items	56	27	13	10	0
Buy a car	25	12	4	6	0

[a]Dependent survivors only.

Table A-14

**Most Frequently Reported Survivor
Uses of Negotiated Life Insurance
Proceeds by the Amount of other[a]
Life Insurance Proceeds Received by
Survivors[b] (% Distribution)**

Most Frequently Reported Uses	No. of Times Reported	$0001- 1999	$2000- 3999	$4000 +
1963				
N =		152	59	36
Savings or investments	133	34%	53%	50%
Pay off mortgage or buy house	98	33	29	22
Purchase household items	71	24	20	25
Buy a car	39	13	12	19
1965				
N =		123	103	87
Savings or investments	183	52%	40%	45%
Pay off mortgage or buy house	94	22	24	26
Purchase household items	56	10	23	11
Buy a car	25	7	9	5

[a]Excluding the amount received from
negotiated Group Life Insurance.
[b]Dependent survivors only.

Table A-15

Most Frequently Reported Uses of Group Life Insurance Proceeds by Widow's without or with Chronic Illness or Long-Standing Condition which Requires Regular Treatment or Care or which is Disabling in any way[a] (% Distribution)

Most Frequently Reported Uses	No. of Times Reported	Proportion Responding	
		Yes	No
1963			
N =		111	211
Savings or investments	126	34%	40%
Pay off mortgage or buy house	95	26	31
Purchase household items	69	24	20
Buy a car	38	9	13
1965			
N =		112	255
Savings or investments	171	36%	47%
Pay off mortgage or buy house	88	20	26
Purchase household items	53	15	14
Buy a car	25	8	6

[a]See note a, Table A-11.

Table A-16

**Most Frequently Reported Survivor
Uses of Group Life Insurance Pro-
ceeds by Widow's Country of Birth[a]
(% Distribution)**

Most Frequently Reported Uses	*No. of Times Reported*	Proportion, By Widow's Country of Birth		
		U. S. A.	*Canada*	*Other*
1963				
N =		288	17	19
Savings or investments	126	37%	59%	47%
Pay off mortgage or buy house	95	31	24	16
Purchase household items	69	23	*	21
Buy a car	38	12	6	11
1965				
N =		320	7	40
Savings or investments	171	45%	29%	60%
Pay off mortgage or buy house	88	25	43	15
Purchase household items	53	15	14	8
Buy a car	25	7	14	5

[a]See note a, Table A-11.

Appendix B
Technical Notes on
Methodology

In Chapter 2 an overview of the basic methodology utilized in the study was presented. The following material is included for those interested in the detailed survey procedures and methodology used.

The Sample

The sampling of a population for survey research purposes is often difficult, costly, and fraught with possible error. In this particular study, however, selection of the sample was simple, quick, and efficient. This was because the total universe of the population under study—that is, male UAW workers in Big Three auto company plants in Detroit Metropolitan area who had died in the years 1963 and 1965—was readily identifiable and could easily be listed. Thus, Ford, Chrysler, and General Motors were each able to provide computer printouts showing the name of every nonretired UAW worker in the covered area who had died during those two years, together with his sex, Social Security number, date of death, name and address of beneficiary, relationship of beneficiary, and amount of insurance—which was directly based on the worker's wage bracket.

From these rosters it was a simple matter to select a systematic sample from the total list, with no clustering or stratification. Since approximately 550 cases were desired from each of the two years, and since there were approximately, 1,000 deaths in 1965 and somewhat fewer in 1963, survivor-beneficiaries of 55% of the 1965 population and 60% of the 1963 population were designated for interview.

Of the 1,098 cases originally selected, 20 were dropped from the sample because the beneficiary lived outside the Detroit area or because the case had already been included in the pretest sample. In consequence, the net assignment consisted of 534 survivors of workers who had died in 1963 and 544 survivors of workers who had died in 1965. This latter group subsequently was reduced to 529 when it was found that 15 of the workers whose names had been drawn were actually salaried employees and not the subject of this study.

The Questionnaire and Pretest

The kinds of information sought in the interview included the following major items:

1. certain background information concerning the deceased worker: his age, education, job category, nationality, and so on;
2. similar data concerning his widow, if one survived;
3. the relationship and major activity (for example, work, school) of the worker's dependents at time of his death;

4. the whereabouts and major activity of those same persons at the time of the interview;
5. costs associated with the worker's death; funeral costs, medical bills, taxes, debts, and so on;
6. insurance and other benefits received after the death;
7. total family income and its sources before and after the fatality;
8. home ownership and place of residence before and after the death of the worker;
9. assets, such as savings, securities and real property, before and after the fatality;
10. present insurance on survivors;
11. the fatality's effects on the children's education;
12. sources of advice on financial matters or family problems;
13. effects of the death on widow's social activities;
14. survivor knowledge of Social Security and group insurance benefits.

Work proceeded on the drafting of a questionnaire during the summer of 1965, and this instrument was pretested in the field in September of that year. (The questionnaire and subschedules used are included in Appendix C.)

While the data from the auto companies indicated that about three-fourths of the survivor beneficiaries would be widows, the remaining cases posed some potential interviewing problems. Some of these beneficiaries were unrelated to the deceased worker; others, such as parents or adult children, may have lived outside his household. There were other cases in which multiple beneficiaries were named—two children, for example, sharing the benefits equally. To determine the extent to which the questions were relevant and answerable in those situations, the pretest sample was deliberately selected so that in only half the cases was the widow the beneficiary, while in the other half the beneficiary or beneficiaries were other relatives or nonrelated persons. The same questionnaire was used for both the 1963 and 1965 groups, and the pretest interviewers were instructed to note carefully any evidence of faulty or difficult recall, or of misinterpretation of any of the items.

Of the 65 cases assigned for pretest, 49 interviews were obtained within a two-week period. A debriefing session was held with the interviewers at which time the questionnaire was discussed item by item. The pretest experience was, in general, highly satisfactory. Of the 65 cases approached, only five refused to be interviewed, and three of these were substitutes for the named beneficiary. Interviewers reported good cooperation and had the impression that the income and expense data reported by respondents were generally accurate. To the extent respondents erred in reporting data, the errors are believed to have been in the direction of overestimation of income.

As a result of the pretest, the wording and order of many questions were amended, and certain items were dropped. Examples of the latter are the worker's hourly wage, job classification, and description of his duties. Respondents were often ignorant of this information and it was decided to rely instead on the worker's skill level as reflected by the wage bracket applicable to his group life insurance amount. Respondents were asked, however, whether to their knowledge, the worker had attained journeyman status as a skilled tradesman—that is, held a journeyman's card in the apprenticeable trade.

The only major change in procedure that seemed called for as a result of pretest experience was the development of a short-form questionnaire for cases in which the worker left no dependent survivors.[a] The pretest was also helpful in suggesting an efficient screening procedure to determine whom to interview when the assigned beneficiary was not available for interview (for example, deceased, moved, too ill) or when she was not the most appropriate respondent (for example, the widow was beneficiary, but the deceased worker's brother handled all financial matters for his sister-in-law).[b]

Interviewer Recruitment, Training and Supervision

Since Detroit is one of the 72 Primary Sampling Units in NORC's master sample of the United States, some ten or twelve interviewers are maintained there on a permanent though part time basis to carry out assignments on periodic national surveys. A resident supervisor is responsible for hiring and training replacements to this staff as necessary and for retraining any of the interviewers whose work may fall below acceptable standards. In addition to this basic staff, another dozen interviewers who had been recruited and trained by NORC for work on past surveys requiring large special samples in Detroit were available for interviewing on this study. Thus, more than half of the 40 interviewers deemed desirable for the study were already experienced in NORC surveys and had performed acceptably in the past.

To round out the required staff, 17 new interviewers were recruited from approximately three times that many applicants. Sources of recruitment included the recommendations of current and former interviewers, independent applications received during the prior year, persons recommended by various

---

[a]In 8 cases (6%) the Short Form Questionnaire was used when a deceased was reported as married. Assuming no error, this could only have been so in a technical sense, that is, married but separated or somehow estranged from his legal wife. Since the beneficiary was not the wife and no dependent was reported, it can be inferred that either interviewer error occurred or that the beneficiary status may not have reflected current family circumstances. In only one such case, however, did the group insurance proceeds go to a nonrelative. The small number of cases involved reduces the significance of any possible error or omission that may result if reporting error is present.

[b]Though not a factor in the pretest, the procedure was extended so that dual beneficiaries within the same immediate family would be regarded as if only one beneficiary received the group insurance proceeds. In the 3 cases where the beneficiary selected a combination of lump sum and monthly income benefits, such beneficiaries were grouped with monthly income recipients, except as noted.

contact agencies such as universities and community organizations, and finally a blind newspaper ad with replies directed to a box number.

Those selected after a personal interview with the supervisor were put through the usual NORC training procedures, which involved the study of training materials, the completion of two interviews on a special Training Questionnaire and a subsequent detailed review of these practice interviews in a personal conference with the supervisor, and finally double interviewing in the field, with the supervisor observing the trainee's work and reviewing it with her later.

All of the 39 interviewers were women, and most were aged 35 to 50. These characteristics are fairly typical of survey research interviewers. Males are seldom interested in part time work of a sporadic nature and in addition are less readily accepted into the respondent's home. Younger women most often are employed full time or must care for small children, while older women often lack the physical stamina required for performing the interviewer's task.

In consultation with the chief investigator, NORC's Field Department in Chicago prepared a 37 page Manual of Field Procedures for the Survivor Income Study, which included background information about the study, detailed step-by-step procedures for contacting and interviewing respondents, and an item-by-item review of the two questionnaire forms. This Manual, together with a copy of the basic questionnaire, was mailed to each of the 39 selected interviewers during the latter part of March and a few days later an all-day briefing session was held with about half the group, followed the next day by a similar session with the other half.

These training sessions were attended by the chief investigator, a consulting director, an NORC field supervisor from Chicago, and by the local Detroit supervisor. In general, they involved a review of the questionnaire and manual and the answering of questions raised by the interviewers, followed by mock interviews in which one of the supervisors would play the role of a respondent. Interviewers were encouraged to study the questionnaire and were paid for six hours of study time.

Interviewers were then given their initial assignments and instructed to return their first two completed interviews to the local supervisor. The supervisor carefully reviewed these early interviews in order to spot any errors, misunderstandings, or weaknesses in the interviewer's work and subsequently moved to correct these either by telephone or in a personal conference. Later interviews were spotchecked for quality control and a random of 10% of the completed interviews were validated by means of a phone call to the respondent. The great majority of interviews were completed during the month of April, though activity on hard-to-find cases continued until mid-May.

Interview Procedure and Completion Rate

Form letters had been prepared and personally addressed to each of the beneficiaries in the sample. The letter on UAW letterhead briefly explained the purpose and sponsorship of the study, informed the beneficiary that an NORC interviewer would shortly ask for an appointment, and assured him or her that all information provided would be kept confidential and would in no way affect the survivor's insurance benefits. Interviewers received these letters, addressed and ready for mailing, along with their materials and posted them several days before they planned to make their calls. Their first personal approach to the respondent was usually by telephone if the number could be ascertained, otherwise by personal visit. The interviewer would refer to the letter, answer any questions or provide any reassurances desired, and then administer a short Screening Questionnaire.

The purpose of the Screening Questionnaire was to make sure that the interviewer was actually talking to the designated beneficiary and that that person was properly the one to interview. Thus, the interviewer would first confirm that the presumed respondent was actually the beneficiary of the deceased auto worker and then confirm his or her relationship to the worker. If the designated beneficiary was the worker's widow, the interviewer then sought to make an appointment for the interview; if the widow could not be interviewed for the reasons of health or prolonged absence from the household, the interviewer was instructed to find out who was the most knowlegeable about her financial affairs and to attempt an interview with that person.

If the designated beneficiary was not the widow, the interviewer asked first whether the worker left any dependent survivors, to determine whether to ask the long or short form of the questionnaire of the dependent survivor; and second whether the designated beneficiary was the best person for me to interview about (worker) or would someone else know more about his insurance benefits and the family's business affairs. If someone else was mentioned as more knowledgeable, the interviewer took that person for his respondent and attempted an interview with him.

Interviewers made every attempt to complete each case assigned. If the respondent was no longer at the designated address, efforts were made to trace him by telephone, certified mail, or inquiry of neighbors. If the respondent was not at home, interviewers made a minimum of two callbacks, and often more, on different days and at different times. Inquiry was sometimes made of neighbors to ascertain the best time to find the respondent at home. In the event of a refusal, interviewers filled out a form detailing the circumstances and ascribed reasons for the refusal; a personal letter was addressed to the refuser, seeking to answer his or her objections to the interview, and a second interviewer was assigned to make a further attempt. Table B-1 shows the number and percentage of interviews completed for the two groups of survivors and the reasons for attrition of the sample originally drawn.

Not surprisingly, a significantly higher completion rate was achieved with the 1965 survivors than with those in the 1963 group. A total of 13% of the earlier group of survivors had either moved out of the Detroit area, were deceased, or could not be traced. Only 3% of the 1965 survivors fell into these categories. (In retrospect, this outcome should have been foreseen and a larger number of 1963 survivors been assigned initially.)

Table B-1

Interview Completion Rate

	1963		1965		Total	
	N	*%*	*N*	*%*	*N*	*%*
Total number of interviews assigned	534	100	544	100	1078	100
Reason for noncompletion						
A. Refused to be interviewed	37	7	35	6	72	7
B. Broke off interview	2	*	2	*	4	*
C. Moved, could not be located	38	7	7	1	45	4
D. Moved out of area	27	5	9	2	36	3
E. Not home after three or more calls	9	2	5	1	14	1
F. Deceased	8	1	1	*	9	1
G. Salaried employee incorrectly assigned	–	–	15	3	15	1
H. Other reasons for noninterview	4	1	6	1	10	1
Number of interviews completed	409	77	464	86	873	82

*less than 0.6%

The overall completion rate of 82% may be regarded as satisfactory. Indeed, if the movers, the deceased, and the incorrect assignments are subtracted from the base of 1,078, it appears that the interviewers successfully interviewed 90% of those survivors available for interview. Other than group insurance benefits (which were comparable), no data were obtained for those not interviewed and included in the test sample. Thus there is little basis for comparing any of the characteristics of those studied and those who could not be interviewed according to the above procedure.

Coding and Data Processing

The questionnaires were largely precoded, so that in most cases interviewers either circled a code number representing the respondent's answer or wrote in a numerical figure. In spite of this precoding, however, a considerable amount of time and effort had to be devoted to office coding and editing. First, there had to be consistency in the numerical or financial data. Editors had to make sure, for example, that the component costs of the funeral equalled the total cost recorded and that expenses reported in one part of the questionnaire were not duplicated in another. Where data were missing or ambiguous, estimates had to be made or the interviewer returned to the field for further information. Second, there were several free-answer questions of the order of "What was the money used for?" or "Why did you move?", for which special codes had to be developed and applied. Finally, a separate IBM card was punched for each dependent survivor in the worker's family, marking his age, education, relationship, and so on, and these data were transcribed from the questionnaire to code sheets.

Once the data were coded and cleaned, they were transferred to magnetic tape and all tabulations were run through NORC's 1401 computer.

Sampling Errors

A large proportion of the universe for the years 1963 and 1965 was included in the sample—the sample was 60% of the population in 1963, 55% of the population in 1965 and 57% for the two years combined.

For this reason, sampling errors will be considerably smaller than those expected from a standard random sample of a smaller fraction of the universe. For 1963, the sampling errors will be 63% of random sampling errors, for 1965, sampling errors will be 67% of random sampling errors, and for the two years combined, sampling errors will be 65% of random sampling errors.[c]

The sample was a systematic sample of the total list of beneficiaries, with no stratification or clustering. Except for the finite correction factor, it may be treated as a simple random sample.

As a convenience to the reader, Table B-2 arrays the sampling errors, with a finite correction factor of .65 included for various sample sizes and percentage splits.[1] For example, reviewing Table 3-2, the 10% short form workers, age 35-44, included in the sample, might (due to sampling error) range from 8.2% to 11.8% in the population. This estimate is obtained by interpolating Table B-2 for a sample size of 138 of which 10% are in the given category.

Detroit City Worker's Family Budget

As indicated in Chapter 2, a standard measure of income adequacy, the Detroit City Worker's Family Budget (DCWFB) was utilized in evaluating the ongoing

---

[c]The *finite correction factor used* in computing sampling error is $\sqrt{1 - \text{sampling fraction}}$.

Table B-2

Percentage Sampling Errors–(1 Sigma)

1963 or 1965

Percentage Split n	50	100	200	300	400	Total 540
5 - 95	2.0	1.4	1.0	0.8	0.7	.6
10 - 90	2.8	2.0	1.4	1.1	1.0	.8
20 - 80	3.7	2.6	1.9	1.5	1.3	.9
30 - 70	4.2	3.0	2.1	1.7	1.5	1.0
40 - 60	4.5	3.2	2.3	1.8	1.6	1.4
50 - 50	4.5	3.2	2.3	1.8	1.6	1.6

1963 and 1965 Combined

Percentage Split n	50	100	200	400	600	800	Total 1,078
5 - 95	2.0	1.4	1.0	0.7	.6	.5	.4
10 - 90	2.8	2.0	1.4	1.0	.8	.7	.6
20 - 80	3.7	2.6	1.9	1.3	1.1	.9	.6
30 - 70	4.2	3.0	2.1	1.5	1.2	1.1	.7
40 - 60	4.5	3.2	2.3	1.6	1.3	1.1	1.0
50 - 50	4.5	3.2	2.3	1.6	1.3	1.2	1.1

Difference between 1963 and 1965

Percentage Split Each n	50	100	200	300	400	Total 540
5 - 95	2.8	2.0	1.4	1.1	1.0	.8
10 - 90	4.0	2.8	2.0	1.6	1.4	1.1
20 - 80	5.2	3.7	2.7	2.1	1.8	1.3
30 - 70	5.9	4.2	3.0	2.4	2.1	1.4
40 - 60	6.4	4.5	3.3	2.5	2.3	2.0
50 - 50	6.4	4.5	3.3	2.5	2.3	2.3

adjustment of the surviving units studied. Table B-3 further describes the measure and summarizes the values utilized in comparison to the incomes reported for the surviving families. Thus, for example, a surviving widow headed family (age 35-54) with 2 children would require an income of $5547 to maintain an equivalent to the modest but adequate standard of living established by the Bureau of Labor Statistics.

It is difficult to establish budget or income figures with which the DCWFB standard utilized may be compared and, in effect, partially validated as a

Table B-3

Detroit City Worker's Family Budget[a]
1966 (1959 Series)
(Adjusted by Detroit Consumer
Price Index)

	Age of Family Head			
	Under 35	*35-54*	*55-64*	*65 +*
One Person[b]	$2427	$2889	$2658	$2138
Two Persons				
H, W; 2A	3640	3813	3871	3640
1P, 1C	3582	3929	3871	3698
Three Persons				
H, W, C (6-15)	4680	5027	5258	4853
1P, 2C	4622	5547	–	–
Four Persons				
H, W, 2C (6-15)	5489	5778[c]	6414	5835
1P, 3C	5893	6934	–	–
Five Persons				
H, W, 3C (6-15)	6644	6934	7626	–
1P, 4C	6703	7106	–	–
Six or More Persons				
H, W, 4+ (6-15)	7569	7916	8494	–
IP, 5C+	7338	7569	–	–

Age of oldest child in parentheses.

[a]Estimated annual cost of goods and services providing the same level of well-being as the basic city worker's family budget for families varying in size, age of head and children, and composition. Though husband-headed families were excluded in evaluating survivor income, some values for such families are provided as a point of reference. The measure used is based on the cost of family consumption; it omits taxes, life insurance, and occupational expenses. For additional description and use, see Chapters 2 and 4. For detail on Budget, see "The Interim City Worker's Family Budget" Helen H. Lamale & Margaret S. Stotz, *Monthly Labor Review,* August, 1960.

A 1966 series updating and modifying the earlier data shows a cost of $7241 for the standard family (see note c); 125% of adjusted 1959 data. The 1966 data were available too late to incorporate in the calculations for this study. (*City Worker's Family Budget for a Moderate Living Standard,* Bureau of Labor Statistics, Bulletin No. 1570-1, U.S. Dept. of Labor.)

H – Husband; W – Wife; A – Adult;
C – Children; P – Parent; + (and over).

[b]For extra adult dependents (over 21 years of age) add 1/2 of one person by age of individual.

[c]Standard CWFB Family. In New York City, ("Annual Price Survey–Family Budget Costs," Budget Standard Service, The Community Council of Greater New York) the October, 1966 cost (without taxes) for a similar family was $6213. Including taxes, the budget standard required $7281. (P. 2)

The cost of a modest but adequate standard of living differs between New York and Detroit. However, the difference indicated further reflects the modesty of the measure used in this study. In 1959, for example, the cost of a modest but adequate standard of living in Detroit was 2% higher than the cost of a similar standard in New York. ("The Interim City Worker's Family Budget," Helen Lamale and Margaret S. Stotz, *Monthly Labor Review),* August, 1960, pp. 787.

standard. The median predeath family income of the families studied and of all auto workers appreciably exceeded this standard for all but the largest families for the years considered. Though taxes are omitted from this standard, their addition would not materially alter the above generalization. Though the DCWFB budget (as modified to reflect rising prices) generally exceeded that applicable to the payments of welfare, few would argue that welfare should be the standard applied to survivors of industrial or other workers.[d]

In sum, however, it is felt by the authors that the DCWFB is essentially a conservative measure of a modest but adequate standard of living. Its application in the study was even more conservative, that is, many who meet the standard as well as those considered to fail in meeting it generally would be acknowledged as having substandard incomes. The conservative application derives from the following factors:

1. While every effort was made to obtain an accurate estimate of survivor income, it is believed that the errors, if any, were generally in the direction of overstating income. While it was not possible to correct for this possible overstatement, it should be considered in evaluating the DCWFB scores reported.
2. The income used is before taxes; however, the budget standard omits taxes. Since much of the survivor income is tax-free and taxes would otherwise vary, it was considered inefficient to calculate and include taxes. Insurance costs are also omitted from the budget used. As many widows reported owning insurance, this is a further conservative element to be recognized.
3. Given the possible error in reporting income and the difficulty of a single budget figure covering all families of a given size and age of head, the DCWFB standard was broadened to encompass a range of $500 in either direction.

An indirect confirmation of the conservative nature of the measure used is derived from the data on a 1966 moderate living standard released in Bureau of Labor Statistics Bulletin No. 1570-1. As an indicator of the differences in the two measures, the budget figure for the standard family, as released in Bulletin 1570-1 is 25% higher than that used in the data on which the present study is based.

---

[d]Actually, the welfare provision of housing prior to 1968 was roughly equivalent (depending on family size) to that included in the DCWFB budget used. This is a further indicator of the conservative nature of the DCWFB measure, as used in the study.

Appendix C
Specimen Interview
Schedules

National Opinion Research Center
University of Chicago

Screening Questionnaire

Case No: _____

Ask to speak to assigned beneficiary. (If assigned beneficiary is not accessible, conduct screening with a responsible adult in the household, but ask the questions *about* the assigned beneficiary.)

Hello, I'm (*your name*) of the National Opinion Research Center. I believe you got a letter recently, explaining that we would like to interview you in connection with the insurance benefits paid to survivors of former (___ _____) workers.   auto

manufacturer

1. I understand you are (a/the) beneficiary of _____
                                                        (worker's) (auto manufacturer)
   _____ life insurance. Is that correct?
   (insurance company)

Yes (Go to Q. 2)	1
Yes, with others (Go to Q. 2)	2
No (Ask A)	3

   A. *If no:* Who is the beneficiary of this insurance? Obtain name, address, and telephone number if possible and enter here. Discontinue screening and contact your supervisor.

2. Now, you are his (_____) (If face sheet says "wife" read
                              relationship to worker
   "widow" here); is that correct? If no, probe for correct relationship. Circle one code below.

Widow (See A)	1
Divorced or separated wife	2
Son or daughter (or in-law)	3
Brother or sister (or in-law)	4
Father or mother (or in-law)	5
Other relative (specify)	6
Nonrelative (specify)	7

   (Go to Q. 3)

   A. *If widow:* Begin *long form* interview with widow, or make appointment.

   If the widow is not accessible;

(1) Determine who is most knowledgeable about widow and her business affairs, and attempt to administer long form interview with that person.

(2) Enter below reason why widow is not interviewed.

3. *If assigned beneficiary is other than widow*

Did (*worker*) leave any survivors—including yourself—who were dependent on him for all or part of their financial support?

Yes (Ask Q. 4 and use the long form interview)   1

No (Ask Q. 4 and use the short form interview)   2

4. Would you be the best person for me to interview about (*worker*) or would someone else know more about his insurance benefits and the family's business affairs?

Assigned Beneficiary (See A)   1

Someone Else (See B)   2

A. *If assigned beneficiary:* Begin interview or make an appointment for interview if assigned beneficiary is accessible.

If assigned beneficiary is not accessible;

(1) try to find another knowledgeable person for interview.

(2) enter below reason why assigned beneficiary is not interviewed.

B. *If other than assigned beneficiary:* Get name, address, phone number, and relationship to worker of person named and enter below:

Name:

Address:

Phone No: Relationship to worker:

Administer a screening interview to person named if accessible.

(1) try to find another knowledgeable person for interview.

(2) enter below reason why person named in B. is not interviewed:

National Opinion Research Center

University of Chicago

Face sheet

Case
Number: _____

Worker's
Name: _____   Date of Death: _____

Plant where
employed _____   Social Security
Number: _____

Name & address of beneficiary   relationship to worker: amount of insurance:

(Name) _____   _____   _____

(Address) _____   _____   _____

(City, State) _____   _____   _____

Other
Beneficiaries _____   _____   _____

_____   _____   _____

Insurance Company	John Hancock.........1
Aetna.............2
Metropolitan Life.....3

Auto Manufacturer:	Ford Motor Co.........1
Chrysler Corp.........2
General Motors Corp...3

Name & Address of person Interviewed:	Relationship to Worker: _____	Sex: _____

(Name) _____

(Address) _____

(City, State) _____

This person was interviewed on: _____	Long Form Interview.............1
Short Form Interview.............2

Record of all calls on this case:

Date Time	Name of person called on	Outcome	Interviewer

Noninterview Report

1. Why were you unable to obtain an interview with the assigned beneficiary or responsible informant? CIRCLE ONE.

Refusal (Answer 2 & 3)	1
Breakoff (Answer 3)	2
No one home (Answer 4)	3
Moved, can't locate (Answer 4)	4
Moved, too distant (Answer 5)	5
Sick, senile	6
Out of town	7
Deceased (Answer 6)	8
Other (Specify)	9

2. *If refusal*: Who refused you?

Beneficiary	1
Other (Who?)	2

3. *If refusal or breakoff, record verbatim reason or comment:*

4. *If no one home or moved, can't locate, explain*:

5. *If moved, too distant, record new address*:

6. *If sick, out of town, deceased or other*: Why could you not interview an informant instead?

7. Comments:

8. Date of This Report:

9. Your Signature:

Survivor Income Study
Long Form—Dependent Survivors[a]

Begin Deck 01 _____

Worker's Name: _____   Case No. _____

Name of Respondent: _____	Is respondent the beneficiary? Yes 1 10/0 No 2
Address of Respondent: _____	Relationship of respondent to worker: 11/0

1963	1	12/0	Time Began: _____	AM
1965	2			PM

1. Can you tell me what was (*worker's*) age at the time of his death? _____
   years

   13-14/yy

If widow, circle code 1; otherwise ask:

2. At the time of his death, was (*worker*) married, widowed, divorced, separated, or was he never married?

   Married ⎫   1   15/0
   Widowed ⎪   2
   Divorced ⎬ (Ask A)   3
   Separated ⎭   4
   Never married   5

   A. *If ever married:* Was he married more than once during his life?
      No, married once   1   16/0
      Yes, twice   2
      Yes, three times   3

3. Were you living in (*worker's*) household at the time of his death?
   Yes   1   17/0
   No   2

4. A. *If ever married to worker (even if divorced or separated at time of death):*
   How long were you married to (*worker*)?   _____ years

   18-19/yy

   B. *If divorced or separated from worker at time of his death:*
   How long had you been divorced or separated at the time of his death?

   _____ years

   20-21/yy

_____

[a]A Short Form Questionnaire was administered when there were no dependent survivors. The worker's demographic characteristics, the nature of his death, the cost of the funeral and the estate settlement were covered briefly in this questionnaire.

If ever married to worker:

5. Since (his death, your divorce, or your separation from him), have you remarried?

Yes (Ask A)	1	22/0
No (Ask B)	2	

    A. *If yes:* How long have you been remarried? Record number of *months*.
                                       _____ 23-24/yy

    B. *If no*: Do you think you will ever get married again?

Definitely	1	25/0
Probably	2	
Probably not	3	
Definitely not	4	
Don't know	5	

6. *Ask everyone except widows*

How often did you see (*worker*) during the last year of his life?

Every day	1	26/0
Once a week or more	2	
Once a month or more	3	
Less than once a month	4	
Not at all	5	

7. *Ask everyone*

Now, if you don't mind, I have to get some background information about (*worker*). Was his death the result of illness or an accident?

Illness (Ask A)	1	27/0
Accident (Ask B)	2	
Other (Specify)	3	
Don't know	4	

    A. *If illness:* What was the cause of death listed on the death certificate? If don't know, probe for most specific answer possible.

Heart disease	1	28/0
Cancer	2	
Stroke	3	
Influenza or pneumonia	4	
Diabetes	5	
Other (Specify)	6	

    B. *If accident:* Did the accident happen at work, or outside the plant on the way to or from work, or somewhere else?

At work	1	29/0
On way to or from	2	
Elsewhere	3	

8. A. Did he have CHA (Metropolitan Hospital and Clinics) or Blue Cross-Blue Shield hospital insurance?

CHA	1	30/0
BC/BS	2	
Don't know	3	

B. Do you now have hospital insurance?

Yes (Ask C & D)	1	31/0
No (Go to Q. 9)	2	

If yes to "B":

C. What kind is that?

CHA	1	32/0
BC/BS	2	
Other (Specify)	3	

D. Do you pay the insurance premium directly to the insurance company, or do you pay through (Ford Motor Company, General Motors, Chrysler Corporation)?

Direct to insurance company	1	33/0
Through Ford/GM/Chrysler	2	
Other (Specify)	3	

9. How many years had (*worker*) worked with the company at the time of his death? If don't know, probe for best guess. _____ years

34-35/yy

10. A. What was the last grade he completed in school?

Eighth grade or less	1	36/0
Some high school	2	
Completed high school	3	
Some college	4	
Completed college	5	
Don't know	6	

B. Did he complete apprenticeship training for a journeyman's card?

Yes	1	37/0
No	2	
Don't know	3	

C. Did he ever take other special courses or vocational training?

Yes	1	38/0
No	2	
Don't know	3	

11. In what country was he born?

U.S.A.	1	39/0
Canada (Ask A & B)	2	
Other (Specify and ask A & B)	3	

If outside U.S.A.:

A. Was he a U.S. citizen?

Yes	1	40/0
No	2	

B. How many years did he live in this country?   _____ years

41-42/yy

12. In what country was his father born?

U.S.A.	1	43/0
Canada	2	
Other (Specify)	3	

13. What was (*worker's*) religious preference?

Protestant (Ask A)	1	44/0
Catholic	2	
Jewish	3	
Other (Specify)	4	
None	5	

    A. *If Protestant:* What denomination?

Baptist	1	45/0
Methodist	2	
Episcopalian	3	
Presbyterian	4	
Lutheran	5	
Congregational	6	
Other (Specify)	7	

14. Was he ever in military service?

Yes (Ask A & B)	1	46/0
No	2	

If yes:

    A. In what years was he in active military service?

1940 to 1946	1	47/0
1949 to 1954	2	
Other (Specify)	3	

B.   Did he have any service-connected disability?

Yes	1	48/0
No	2	
Don't know	3	

Ask Q's 15-24 about surviving widow. If you are interviewing widow, ask in terms of "you." If widow survives and you are interviewing someone else, ask in terms of e.g., "your mother," "your sister," "Mrs. ___ " and probe for best information possible.

If no widow survives, skip to Q. 25.

15. A.   What is your (*widow's*) age?   _____ 49-50/yy

     B.   And can I have your (her) Social Security Number?

_____	1	51/0
No Social Security Number	2	
Don't know	3	

16. *If widow survives, but you are interviewing someone else.*
How long was (*widow*) married to (*worker*)? Probe for best guess.

            _____ years
            52-53/yy

17. In what country were you (was *widow*) born?

U.S.A.	1	54/0
Canada (Ask A & B)	2	
Other (Specify and ask A & B)	3	

If outside U.S.A.:
A.   Are you (Is *widow*) a U.S. citizen?

Yes	1	55/0
No	2	

B.   How many years have you (has she) lived in this country?

            _____ years
            56-57/yy

18. In what country was your (*widow's*) father born?

U.S.A.	1	58/0
Canada	2	
Other (Specify)	3	

19. What is your (*widow's*) religious preference?

Protestant	1	59/0
Catholic	2	
Jewish	3	
Other (Specify)	4	
None	5	

    A. *If Protestant:* What denomination?

Baptist	1	60/0
Methodist	2	
Episcopalian	3	
Presbyterian	4	
Lutheran	5	
Congregational	6	
Other (Specify)	7	

20. A. What was the last grade you (*widow*) completed in school?

Eighth grade or less	1	61/0
Some high school	2	
Completed high school	3	
Some college	4	
Completed college	5	

    B. Did you (*widow*) ever take special courses or vocational training?

Yes (Ask C)	1	62/0
No	2	

    C. *If yes to B:* What kind of courses or training was that?

Office	1	63/0
Teaching	2	
Nursing	3	
Beautician	4	
Other (Specity)	5	

21. Were you (Was *widow*) working at the time of (*worker's*) death?

Yes, full time (Ask A)	1	64/0
Yes, part time (Ask A)	2	
No	3	

    A. *If yes: What kind of work was that? Code in column A under Q. 22.*

22. Are you (Is *widow*) working now?

Yes, full time (Ask A)	1	65/0
Yes, part time (Ask A)	2	
No	3	

A. *If yes:* What kind of work is that? Code in column B below.

	A. Then	B. Now
Medical or other health work	1 66/0	1 67/0
Social work, teaching, and kindred	2	2
Manager, official, proprietor	3	3
Clerical and kindred	4	4
Retail sales and other service work	5	5
Craftsman, foreman, and kindred	6	6
Beautician, cosmetologist, and hairdresser	7	7
Domestic service work	8	8
Labor and nonskilled factory work	9	9

23. *Ask only if no to both Q. 21 and Q. 22*
Were you (Was *widow*) ever employed outside the home prior to (*worker's*) death?

Yes (Ask A & B)	1	68/0
No	2	
Don't know	3	

If yes:

A. How many years has it been since you were (*widow* was) last employed? _____ years
                                          69-70/yy

B. What sort of work did you (*widow*) do then?

Medical or other health work	1	71/0
Social work, teaching, and kindred	2	
Manager, official, and proprietor	3	
Clerical and kindred	4	
Retail sales and other service work	5	
Craftsman, foreman, and kindred	6	
Beautician, cosmetologist, and hairdresser	7	
Domestic service work	8	
Labor and nonskilled factory work	9	
Don't know	X	

24. Do you (Does *widow*) have any chronic illness or long-standing condition which requires regular treatment or care or which is disabling in any way?

Yes (Ask A)	1	72/0
No	2	

A. *If yes:* Are you (Is she) considered disabled under the provisions of the Social Security Law?

Yes	1	73/0
No	2	
Don't know	3	

25. Now I would like some information about other members of the family.
    A. What members of (*worker's*) household were dependent on him for at least half their support at the time of his death? Do not list worker or widow, but enter name and relationship to worker of all other dependent members of household in columns on opposite page, e.g., "daughter," "mother," "grandson," etc. If none, circle code below.

    None   1

    B. Did (*worker*) have any other dependents, living away from home?—that is, persons who were dependent on him for at least half their support? If yes, list in succeeding columns on opposite page. If none, circle code below. If more than four, use extra sheet. If respondent is included in list, identify him with an "r" after his name.

    None   2

If none to both A and B, skip to Q. 29.

26. *For each person listed:*
    A. Circle "in" (lived *in* household) or "out" (lived *out*side) on line A

    B. Was (*person*) entirely or only partly dependent on worker for financial support? Circle "all" if person was dependent on worker for *all* financial support or "partly" if *partly* dependent, on line B

    C. What was (*person's*) age at the time of (*worker's*) death? Enter age on line C

    Ask D–I for each person who was 14 or older

    D. Was (*person*) single, married, widowed, divorced, or separated? Circle "S," "M," "W," "D," or "Sep" on line D
    If married, widowed, divorced, or separated, ask E.

    E. *If ever married:* Did (he/she) have any children? Enter number of children on line E. If none, enter "0."

    F. Was (*person*) working, looking for work, going to school, keeping house, retired, or what? Enter on line F.
    If employed or student, ask G.

G. *If employed or student:* Was (*person*) (working/going to school) full time or part time? Circle "full" (full time) or "part" (part time) on line G.

H. What was the last grade (*person*) had completed in school, at that time? Record on line H.

I. At that time, had (*person*) ever taken or was (*person*) taking any courses or vocational training? Circle yes or no on line I.

10/	11/	12/	13/	14/	15/	16/	17/	18/	19/
20/	21/	22/	23/	24/	25/	26/	27/	28/	29/

_____(Name)_____(Name)_____(Name)_____(Name)

(Relationship to worker) | (Relationship to worker) | (Relationship to worker) | (Relationship to worker)

In   Out | In   Out | In   Out | In   Out

All   Partly | All   Partly | All   Partly | All   Partly

Age _____ | Age _____ | Age _____ | Age _____

S M W D Sep | S M W D Sep | S M W D Sep | S M W D Sep

No. children | No. children | No. children | No. children

_____ | _____ | _____ | _____

Full   Part | Full   Part | Full   Part | Full   Part

Yes   No | Yes   No | Yes   No | Yes   No

Transfer names from previous page to corresponding columns on page 11.

27. *For each person listed, ask A and B.*
And now I'd like to know about these same people now.

    A. Does (*person*) live with (any *beneficiary*) now? Circle "yes" or "no" on line A.

    B. Is (*person*) now partly or entirely dependent on (*beneficiary*) for financial support? Enter "all" if person is dependent for *all* financial support, "partly" if *partly* dependent, and "no" if *not* dependent on beneficiary, on line B.
If no, ask C.

    C. *If not dependent on beneficiary:* Who supports (him/her) now? Enter "self" for *self*-supporting, or specify on Line C.

Ask D-H for each person who was 14 or older at time of death.
    D. What is (*person's*) marital status now? Circle "S," "M," "W," "D," or "Sep" on line D.

    E. Is (*person*) working, looking for work, going to school, keeping house, retired, or what? Enter on line E.
If employed or student, ask F.

    F. *If employed or student:* Is that full time or part time? Circle "full" or "part" on line F.

    G. Has (*person*) had any additional schooling since (*worker's*) death? If no, enter "no" on line G. If yes, ask: What is the last grade (he/she) has completed in school? And enter on line G.

    H. Has (*person*) taken or is (*person*) now taking any special courses or vocational training since (*workers's*) death? Circle "yes" or "no" on line H.

28. Do any of the persons we have talked about (from chart) have any chronic illness or long-standing condition, which requires regular treatment or care, or which is disabling in any way?

                  Yes (ask A & B)   1
                  No (go to Q. 29)   2
If yes:
    A. Who is that? Anybody else? Enter "disabled" on line I

    B. Is (*each person mentioned in A*) considered disabled under the provisions of the Social Security Law? Circle "yes" or "no" or "DK" on line J.

30/	31/	32/	33/	34/	35/	36/	37/	38/	39/
40/	41/	42/	43/	44/	45/	46/	47/	48/	49/

(Name)	(Name)	(Name)	(Name)
Yes No	Yes No	Yes No	Yes· No
S M W D Sep	S M W D Sep	S M W D Sep	S M W D Sep
Full Part	Full Part	Full Part	Full Part
Yes No	Yes No	Yes No	Yes No
Yes No	Yes No	Yes No	Yes No
DK	DK	DK	DK

160

Office Use Only_____
(50-54)

29. *Ask only if widow survives*
Is there anyone (else) who is dependent upon you (*widow*) for financial support now? (Anyone that we have not already mentioned?)

Yes (ask A & B)	1	55/0
No	2	

If yes: Ask A & B for each, and record below.
A. What is that person's relationship to you (*widow*)?
B. What is the person's age?

Relationship		*Age*	
_____	*56/y*	_____	*57-58/yy*
_____	*59/y*	_____	*60-61/yy*
_____	*62/y*	_____	*63-64/yy*

30. Now we would like to know as accurately as possible the various expenses associated with (*worker's*) death. First the funeral expenses. If "don't know" to any of the items, probe for best guess. If no expense, enter zero.

Begin deck 0:

_____

EXPENSES

A. What was the cost of the casket? $ _____ 10-13/yyy

B. The burial vault? _____ 14-17/yyy

C. What were the cemetery charges? _____ 18-21/yyy

D. And how much was paid for the grave marker? _____ 22-25/yyy

E. Any tips, or honorariums, to the clergyman or others? How much did that come to, approximately? _____ 26-29/yyy

F. How about the hearse or limousines or transportation to the cemetery? _____ 30-33/yyy

G. How much did the mortician or undertaker charge for his services (for other than those things we already talked about)? _____ 34-37/yyy

H. (If respondent cannot itemize, get total undertaker's bill here.) _____ 38-41/yyy

I. Were there any other charges connected with the funeral that you remember? (If yes, specify and enter amount.) _____ 42-45/yyy

J. Add items A-I and enter total. So the total costs connected with the funeral were about (Read total). Does that sound about right? If no, make necessary corrections. $_____ 46-49/yyy
(TOTAL)

Begin deck 04

31. Now how about medical expenses that had to be paid *after* (*worker's*) death? For each item below, probe for total amount paid by beneficiary or worker's family. If none, enter zero.

Amount paid by Family

A. Were there hospital charges to be paid after (*worker*) died? (What was the total hospital bill that you [the family] had to pay then, not counting anything paid by insurance?) $ _____ 10-13/yyyy

B. How about doctor bills that had to be paid after (*worker*) died? (What was the total amount of these doctor bills, not counting anything paid by insurance?) _____ 14-17/yyyy

C. Were there any other medical expenses that had to be paid after (*worker*) died—such as bills for nurses, medicines, or nursing home care?
Nurses _____ 18-21/yyyy
Medicines _____ 22-25/yyyy
Nursing home care _____ 26-29/yyyy
Other (Specify) _____ 30-33/yyyy

D. Add items A-C and enter total. So the total
of hospital and medical expenses that had to
be paid *after* (*worker's*) death came to about
(read total). Right? If not, make appropriate
corrections. $ _____ 34-37/yyyy

32. How about taxes—were there any estate or inheritance or other taxes
associated with (*worker's*) death?

Yes (ask A & B)	1	38/0
No (go to Q. 33)	2	

If yes:

A. What kind of taxes were these? Circle as many as apply.

Estate	1	39/0
Inheritance	2	
Other (specify)	3	

B. How much did these taxes amount to altogether?

$ ____ 40-43/yyyy

Begin deck 05

33. And costs of estate administration—

Expenses

A. Were there attorney or administrator fees?

(How much?) If none, enter zero $ ____ 10-13/yyy

B. Any other bills or fees in connection with
the estate? If yes, specify kind and amount.   ____ 14-17/yyy

$ ____ 18-21/yyy
(TOTAL)

34. A. Did (*worker*) or his family) have any loans   Amount Owed
or notes payable that were owed at the time
of his death (not counting mortgage on
home)? *If yes:* What was the total amount
owed on these loans? If none, enter zero. $ ____ 22-26/yyy

B. *Ask only if yes to A:* Were these loans from
a bank, a loan company, a credit union,

from a relative or a frined or who? Circle as many as apply.

Bank	1
Loan company	2
Credit union	3
Relative	4
Friend	5
Other (Specify)	6

C. Was money owed on any major installment purchases at the time, such as a car or television, or household appliance? If yes, specify item, source of financing, and amount owed on each at time of death. Use code numbers for credit sources as given in "B" above.

Amount

$ _____ 30-34/yyy

_____ 37-41/yyyy

_____ 44-48/yyyy

Item	28/y	Source of Financing	29/y
	35/y		36/y
	42/y		43/y

D. Were there any other personal debts or obligations that you (the family) had to meet (like unpaid property taxes, etc.)? If yes, specify kind and amount.

$ ——— 49-53/yyy

Enter total of items A-D $ _____ 54-58/yyy

(TOTAL)

35. Were there any other expenses associated with (*worker's*) death that you recall—any other expenses at all? If yes, specify and probe for amounts. If no, enter zero.

Nature of Expense	*Amount*
_____	$ _____
_____	_____
_____	_____ 59-63/yyy

(TOTAL)

Total the amounts from Q's 30-35 and say: So the total of funeral and medical bills, taxes, and other obligations you had to pay *after* (*worker's*) death comes to (Read total). Does that sound about right? If no, probe for corrections and make appropriate changes.

Total Post-Death Expenses $ _____ 64-68/yyy

36. Have all of these expenses been completely paid off, mostly paid off, are many still outstanding, or what?

Completely paid off	1	7/0
Mostly paid off	2	
Many outstanding (Ask A)	3	
Other (Specify)	4	

  A. *If not entirely paid:* How much (of the *total*) is still outstanding?

$ _____ 8-12/yyyyy

37. Did you (the family) have to borrow money from anyone or take out any sort of loan in order to meet any of these expenses associated with the death?

Yes (ask A & B)	1	13/0
No	2	

If yes:

  A. About how much did you (the family) have to borrow?

$ _____ 14-18/yyyyy

  B. Where did you turn for that money?

Credit union	1	19/0
Bank	2	
Loan company	3	
Relative	4	
Friend	5	
Other (Specify)	6	

38. *Ask either A or B in every case*

  A. *Ask 1963 survivors:* At the plant (*worker*) had group life insurance under (John Hancock/Aetna/Metropolitan) which provided either a lump sum cash payment or monthly installments to his survivors. How did you (*beneficiary*) take the life insurance payment—in a lump sum or as the optional monthly installments? Circle code below.

B. *Ask 1965 survivors:* In addition to the $100-a-month Transition benefit available to survivors under (*worker's*) (John Hancock/Aetna/ Metropolitan) group life insurance policy at the plant, the policy also provides either a lump sum cash payment or monthly installments to the survivors. Not talking about the Transition benefit now, but how did you (*beneficiary*) take the regular life insurance payment—in a lump sum or as the optional monthly installments? Circle code below.

Lump sum (ask Q. 39)   1   20/0

Monthly installments (ask Q. 40)   2

39. *If regular insurance payment taken in lump sum*
A. We understand you (beneficiary) received $ _____ in a lump sum. Is that right?   (amount of insurance)

Yes (go to C)   1   26/

No (ask B)   2

B. *If no to A:* How much did you (*beneficiary*) receive?
$ _____ 27-31/yyyyy

C. How much of this lump sum payment was used for expenses associated with (*worker's*) death?
$ _____ 32-36/yyyy

Ask unless *all* of payment was used for expenses of worker's death:
D. What else was the money used for? (And what was done with the rest of it?)

E. How much money is left now from the lump-sum payment?
$ _____ 38-42/yyyyy

40. *If regular insurance payment taken in monthly installments*
A. How much do you (does *beneficiary*) receive in each monthly installment? $ _____ 43-45/yyy

B. Altogether, how many months will you (*beneficiary*) receive these installments?   _____ months
46-47/yy

41. Did you (*beneficiary*) know that you had a choice—that is, that you could take the life insurance benefit either as a lump sum or in monthly installments?

Yes (ask A)   1   48/0

No (ask B & C)   2

A. *If yes:* Why did you (*beneficiary*) take the benefit (in a lump sum/as monthly installments—Q. 38)? (What kinds of things made you decide to take it that way instead of the other?) Any other reason?

If no:
B. If you (*beneficiary*) had known at the time that (you/he) had a choice, do you think (you/he) would have taken the benefit in a lump sum or in monthly installments?

Lump sum	20	50/0
Monthly installments	2	
Don't know (go to Q. 42 instruction)		3

C. Why do you feel that way? Any other reasons?

51/y

42. *Ask widows only*
Did you and your husband ever discuss how this insurance money should be used?

Yes	1	52/0
No	2	

43. *Ask only if death was result of accident (Q. 7)*
How much did you (*beneficiary*) receive from (John Hancock/Aetna/ Metropolitan) as an accidental death benefit? $ _____ 53/57/yyyyy

44. Under Social Security, a lump-sum death benefit of up to $225 is provided. Did you (*beneficiary*) apply for this?

Yes (go to Q. 45)	1	58/0
No (ask A)	2	

A. *If no:* Did anyone else apply for it? (If yes, find out who applied—relationship to worker.)

59/0

45. Under certain conditions, dependent survivors are entitled to monthly benefits under Social Security. Did you (or anyone) apply for these monthly benefits?

Yes (ask A)	1	60/0
No (ask D below)	2	

A. *If yes:* Are you (*the dependent survivors*) receiving these benefits?

Yes (ask B)	1	61/0
No (ask C)	2	

B. *If yes to A:*
How much do you (they) receive from Social Security each month?
$ _____ 62-64/yyy

C. *If no to A:*
Why aren't you (they) receiving Social Security benefits?

Application not yet processed	1	65/0
Not eligible until older	2	
Not eligible, other reasons (Specify)	3	
Other (Specify)	4	
Don't know	5	

D. *If no to first part of Q. 45:* Why did you (or anyone) not apply?

Knew not eligible till older	1	66/0
Never got around to applying	2	
Don't need it, don't believe in it	3	
Other (Specify)	4	

46. *Ask only if applied for Social Security benefits (Yes to Q. 44 or Q. 45):*
Did anyone help you (*person applying*) apply for these Social Security benefits?

Yes (ask A & B)	1	67/0
No (go to Q. 47)	2	

If yes: *If yes:*
A. Who helped you (*person applying*) apply? Circle as many as appropriate.

Attorney	1	68/0
Businessman	2	
Local Social Security Office	3	
Company representative	4	
Union representative	5	
Mortician or undertaker	6	
Insurance man	7	
Social worker	8	
Other (Specify)	9	

B. Did any of the people who helped charge for this help?

Yes (ask C & D)	1	69/0
No (go to Q. 47)	2	

If yes to B:
C. Who charged for this help? Enter code number(s) from "A" above.
$ _____ 70/0
D. Altogether, how much did (he/they) charge?
$ _____ 71-79/yyy

168

47. We're interested in any other financial or material help the dependent
survivors might have received after (*worker's*) death. For example, did
(you/they) receive benefits from any of these sources? Hand respondent
card A. Circle code for each one mentioned; then ask appropriate
supplement for *each one* mentioned.

	Yes	Ask Supplement
A. Workmen's Compensation	1	A (Blue)
B. Public Liability	2	B (Orange)
C. Veterans' Insurance	3	C (Yellow)
D. Private Life Insurance	4	D (White)
E. Cridit Union Life Insurance	5	E (Green)
F. Mortgage Retirement Insurance	6	F (Goldenrod)
G. Credit Insurance	7	F (Goldenrod)
H. Fraternal Order or Lodge (Specify)	8	D (White)
I. Travel Accident Insurance	9	D (White)
J. Any Other Insurance (Specify)	X	D (White)
None	0	

48. *If any item coded "yes" in Q. 47*
Did anyone help you (*person applying*) apply for (*benefits coded "yes" in Q. 47*)?

Yes (ask A & B)	1	8/0
No (go to Q. 49)	2	

If yes:

A. Who helped you (*person applying*) apply? Circle as many as appropriate.

Attorney	1	9/0
Businessman	2	
Local Social Security office	3	
Company representative	4	
Union representative	5	
Mortician or undertaker	6	
Insurance man	7	
Social worker	8	
Other (Specify)	9	

B. Did any of the people who helped charge for this help?

Yes (ask C & D)	1	10/0
No (go to Q. 49)	2	

If yes to B:

C. Who charged for this help? Enter code number(s) from "A" above.

$ _____ 11/0

D. Altogether, how much did (he/they) charge? $ _____ 12-14/yyy

49. It's important for us to know what *other* sources of income (the family/dependent survivors) had during the twelve months *before* (*worker's*) death. For example ... Ask each item below. If none or doesn't apply, enter zero. If yes, enter approximate total amount.

Approximate
Total

A. *Ask of or about widow:* Were you (Was *widow*) working? If yes, ask: What were (your/her) total earnings during that 12-month period? $ _____ 15-18/yyy

B. Were any of the (other) dependents con-tributing to the family income? If yes, enter approximate total amount next to appropriate category.
Children $ _____ 19-22/yyyy
Parents _____ 23-26/yyyy
Other relative (Specify) _____ 27-30/yyyy

C. Was financial assistance received from any other family member or friend during that period? If yes, enter total amount next to appropriate source.
Family member $ _____ 31-34/yyyy
Friend _____ 35-38/yyyy

D. Did the family have any other income, such as from rental property, or interest from stocks or savings bonds, or anything else? If yes, enter total amount next to appropriate source of income.
Rental property $ _____ 39-42/yyyy
Interest _____ 43-46/yyyy
Other (Specify) _____ 47-50/yyyy

Enter total of all items in A-D: $ _____ 51-55/yyyyy

50. Was (*worker*) off sick at any time for more than a week during the twelve months before his death?

Yes (ask A-E)	1	56/0
No (go to Q. 51)	2	

If yes:

A. *Ask only if some income listed on page 21; if none, go to C*
Would the other income we were talking about, besides (*worker's*) own earnings, have been received anyhow, if (*worker*) had not been off sick? (For example, would (you) (or the children) have worked even if he had not been off sick?)

Yes, even if not sick (ask C)	1	57/0
Yes generally, but source or amount amount would have differed (ask B)	2	
No (askC)	3	

B. *If "yes generally" to "A":* How would it have been different?

58/y

C. How many weeks was (*worker*) off sick during the twelve months before his death? (Approximately)

_____ weeks   59/60yy

D. Did he receive any weekly benefits through the plant (John Hancock/Aetna/Metropolitan) Sickness and Accident Insurance during that time?

Yes	1	61/0
No	2	
Don't know	3	

E. *Ask survivors of Chrysler employees only:* Did he receive any monthly installment payments from the plant insurance because of a Permanent and Total Disability during the last twelve months before his death?

Yes (ask F & G)	1	62/0
No	2	

If yes:
F. How much money did he receive through the plant Permanent and Total Disability Plan during that period? $ _____ 63-66/yyyy

G. How many months did he receive these payments?

_____ months   67-68/yy

Leave blank.
Total annual income reported deck 07: $ _____ 69-73/yyyyy

51. Now let's consider the (dependent survivors') regular family income at the present time, excluding (*worker's*) insurance policy and his Social Security.

Approximate
Weekly
Amount

A. *If widow is working (Q. 22):* How much do you (does *widow*) earn each week, on the average, before taxes and other deductions? $ _____ 7-9/yyy

B. Do any (other) dependents contribute to the (dependent survivors') family income? Enter approximate weekly amount next to category of relationship to worker. If none, enter zero.
Children $ _____ 10-12/yyy
Parents   _____ 13-15/yyy
Other relatives (Specify)   _____ 16-18/yyy

C. Are you (the dependent survivors) receiving income from any other family member or friend? If yes, enter weekly amount next to appropriate category.
Family member $ _____ 19-21/yyy
Friend   _____ 22-24/yyy

D. Do you (the dependent survivors) have any other income, such as from rental property, interest from stocks or savings bonds, your (their) own Social Security, or anything else—not counting insurance? If yes, enter weekly amount next to appropriate category.
Rental property $ _____ 25-27/yyy
Interest   _____ 28-30/yyy
Other (Specify)   _____ 31-33/yyy

Enter total of all items A-D: $ _____ 34-37/yyyy

If 1963, skip to Q. 55

52. *Ask only of or about 1965: (1) widows; (2) unmarried children under 21; or (3) dependent parents who received at least 50 percent support from worker*

Are you (Is *widow, child, parent*) receiving, or have (you/they) applied for the $100-per-month Transition Benefit, which is an added benefit of the (John Hancock/Aetna/Metropolitan) life insurance?

Yes, now receiving it (ask A)	1	43/0
Yes have applied for it (ask A)	2	
No (ask B)	3	

A. *If yes:* For how many months is this Transition Benefit paid?

_____ months 44-46/yyy

B. *If no: Why not?*

47/y

53. *Ask only of or about 1965 widows*
   A. How old were you (was *widow*) at the time of (your/her) husband's death?

Age ____ 48-49/yy

   B. *Ask only of or about widows aged 50-61 at time of husband's death:* Will you (*widow*) be eligible for any further insurance benefit from (your/her) husband's plant life insurance after the Transition Benefit is exhausted?

Yes (ask C-D)	1	50/0
No	2	
Don't know	3	

If yes:
   C. How much money will this benefit pay?

$100 per month	1	51/0
Other (Specify)	2	

   D. And for how long will these payments continue? Code as many as mentioned.

As long as no Social Security	1	52/0
Until remarriage	2	
Until age 62	3	
Don't know	4	

54. *Ask 1965 survivors only:* During the next six months or so, do you (dependent survivors) expect to have any other income that you (they)

don't have now? If yes, specify source of income and approximate weekly amount.

Source of extra income   *Weekly Amount*

_____ $ _____ 53-55/yyy
_____   _____ 56-58/yyy

Leave blank. Total weekly income reported in deck 08:
                                                   $ _____ 59-63/yyyyy

55. Before (*worker's*) death, did he own or rent his home?
                Own (ask A & B)   1   10/0
                Rent (ask E & F)   2
                Other (Specify)   3

If own:
A. About how much would the home have sold for on the market?
                                    $ _____ 11-15/yyyyy

B. Was it owned free and clear, or was there a mortgage?
                Free and clear (Go to Q. 56)   1   16/0
                Mortgage (Ask C & D)   2

If Mortgage:
C. About how much was still owed at the time? $ _____ 17-21/yyyyy

D. And how much were the monthly payments on the mortgage, including interest, taxes, and insurance? $ _____ 22-24/yyy

If rent:
E. Did he rent a house or apartment?
                House   1   25/0
                Apartment   2

F. About how much was the monthly rent? $ _____ 26-28/yyy

56. *Ask only of or about widow if living now*
Do you (does *widow*) still live in the same home that you (she) lived in at that time?
                Yes (Ask appropriate ABC)   1   29/0
                No (Go to Q. 57)   2

If yes:
A. *If home owned (Q.55):* About how much would the home sell for today? $ _____ 30-34/yyyyy

B.   *If home mortgaged (Q. 55-B):*
  (1) About how much do you (does she) still owe on the house?
  $ _____ 35-39/yyyyy
  (2) How much are your (her) monthly payments?
  $ _____ 40-42/yyy
  (3) Do you (Does *widow*) meet the mortgage payments (yourself/ herself), or does someone else pay it for (you/her)?
  Widow   1   43/0
  Someone else (Specify relationship) 2

C.   *If home rented (Q. 55):*
  (1) How much is the monthly rent today? $ _____ 44-46/yyy
  (2) Do you (Does widow) pay the rent (yourself/herself), or does someone else pay it for (you/her)?
  Widow   1   47/0
  Someone else (Specify relationship) 2

Now skip to Q. 58

57. *Ask only if no to Q. 56*
  A.   Why did you (*widow*) move?

  48/y

  B.   Do you (Does *widow*) own or rent (your/her) present home?
  Own (Ask C & D)   1   49/0
  Rent (Ask H-J)   2
  Other (Specify)   3

  If own:
  C.   About how much would the home sell for on today's market?
  $ _____ 50-54/yyyyy

  D.   Do you (Does *widow*) own it free and clear, or is there a mortgage?
  Free and clear (Go to Q. 58)   1   55/0
  Mortgage (Ask E-G)   2

  If mortgage:
  E.   About how much do you (does *widow*) still owe on the house?
  $ _____ 56-60/yyyyy

F. How much are the monthly payments, including interest, taxes, and insurance? $ _____ 61-63/yyy

G. Do you (Does *widow*) meet the mortgage payments (yourself/herself), or does someone else pay it for (you/her)?

Widow	1	64/0
Someone else (Specify relationship)	2	

If rent:

H. Do you (Does she) rent a house or an apartment?

House	1	65/0
Apartment	2	

I. How much rent do you (does she) pay each month?
                                                                $ _____ 66-68/yyy

J. Do you (Does *widow*) pay the rent (yourself/herself), or does someone else pay it for (you/her)?

Widow	1	69/0
Someone else (Specify relationship)	2	

BEGIN DECK 10

58. A. At the time of (*worker's*) death, did the family (*dependent survivors*) have any cash savings such as a savings or checking account in a bank, or savings deposited in a savings and loan company or credit union? Code on line A below.

B. Did the family have any securities such as U.S. Savings Bonds, mutual fund shares, or stocks? Code on line B below.

If yes to either A or B, ask: About how much did the (savings account and/or securities) amount to altogether? Enter below.

C. Did the family have real property of any kind (other than the home)? Code below. *If yes, ask:* What was the approximate value? Enter below.

D. And did the family have any interest in a business? Code below. *If yes, ask:* What was the approximate value of that? Enter below.

	Yes	No	Don't Know		Approximate Value
A. Cash savings	1	2	3	7/0	$ ___ 9-13/yyyyy
B. Securities	1	2	3	8/0	
C. Real property	1	2	3	14/0	$ ___ 15-19/yyyyy
D. Interest in a business	1	2	3	20/0	$ ___ 21-25/yyyyy

E. *Enter total value of A-D:* So that, at the time of (*worker's*) death, the family had approximately (TOTAL) altogether. Is that right? If not, make appropriate corrections.

Total of above: $ ___ 21-25/yyyyy

59. And now today—Thinking of all the assets we've just mentioned—cash savings, securities, real property, or interest in a business—and adding them up, how would you say the total compares with the total at the time of (*worker's*) death? Would you say it's much more today, a little more, about the same, a little less, or much less than it was then?

Much more (Ask A)	1	32/0
A little more	2	
About the same	3	
A little less	4	
Much less (Ask A)	5	
Don't know	6	

A. *If much more or much less:*
Can you tell me what mainly accounts for the change?

33/y

34/y

60. Who usually handled the money in your (*worker's*) family before his death? That is, who kept track of the bills and paid them?

Worker	1	35/0
Widow	2	
Both	3	
Other (Specify)	4	

61. *If no widow or dependent children, skip to Q. 63*
Did you (*widow*) and/or children carry any sort of life insurance on (your/their) own lives, at the time of (*worker's*) death?

Yes (Ask A-C)	1	36/0
No (Go to Q. 62)	2	
Don't know (Go to Q. 62)	3	

If yes:
A. Who was that?

Widow only	1	37/0
Widow and children	2	
Children only	3	

B. Do (you/they) still carry this insurance?

Yes, all	1	38/0
Some dropped (Ask C)	2	
No, all dropped (Ask C)	3	
Don't know	4	

C. *If any dropped:* Why did (you/they) discontinue it?

Could not afford to keep up payments	1	39/0
Not needed any more, no dependents	2	
Other (Specify)	3	
Don't know	4	

62. Have you (*widow*) and/or dependent children taken out any (other) life insurance since then?

Yes (Ask A-F)	1	40/0
No (Go to Q. 63)	2	

If yes:
A. Who is covered by this insurance?

Widow only	1	41/0
Widow and children	2	
Children only	3	

B. What kind of new insurance do you (*widow/children*) have? Ask separately for widow/children, code as many as apply for each.

	Widow		Children	
Term life	1	42/0	1	43/0
Ordinary life with cash value	2		2	
Endowment	3		3	
Other (Specify)	4		4	
Don't know	5		5	

C. What was the main reason for taking out your (*widow's/children's*) policy? Ask and record separtely for widow/children as applicable.

Widow	*Children*	
		44/y
		45/y

D. How are your (*widow's/children's*) insurance premiums paid—does a company agent call to collect, or is the money always sent to the company(s)? Ask and record separately.

	Widow		Children	
Agent calls to collect	1	46/0	1	47/0
Money sent to the company	2		2	
Don't know	3		3	

E. Did you (*widow/children*) get the new insurance from the same company that handled (*worker's*) group insurance at the plant, or from a different company? Ask and record separately.

	Widow		Children	
Same company	1	48/0	1	49/0
Different company	2		2	
Don't know	3		3	

F. *Refer to Q. 47. Ask only if worker had additonal private life insurance:* Did you (*widow/children*) get this new insurance from the same company that handled (*worker's*) private insurance, or from a different company altogether? Ask and record separately.

	Widow		Children	
Same company	1	50/0	1	51/0
Different company	2		2	
Don't know	3		3	

63. After (*worker's*) death, did you (*dependent survivors*) find it necessary to cut down on living expenses in any way?

Yes (Ask A)	1	52/0
No (Ask B)	2	

A. *If yes:* What sort of things did you cut down on? Anything else?

53-54/yy

B. *If no:* What was the main reason (you/they) did not have to cut down on expenses?

55/y

If no widow and no dependent children, end interview here. If widow but no children, go to Q. 66.

Ask Q's 64-65 only if one or more dependent children under 18 were living in worker's household at time of death (Q. 25, P. 8).

64. Now some questions about the child(ren).

			(1) Before Fatality	(2) Present Time
A. (1) How well were the children doing in school before (*worker's*) death—very well, fairly well, or not so well? Code in col. (1). (2) And how about now? Code in col. (2).	Very well	1 56/0	1 57/0
	Fairly well	2	2
	Not so well	3	3
	Pre-school	4	4
	Don't know	5	5
B. (1) How often did the children visit in friends' homes or have friends visit them before (*worker's*) death? (2) And how about now?	2-3 times week	1 58/0	1 59/0
	Once a week	2	2
	2-3 times month	3	3
	Less often	4	4
	Never	5	5
C. (1) And how often did the children take part in group activities with other children, like plays, scouting, sports, and so on, before? (2) And how about now?	2-3 times week	1 60/0	1 61/0
	Once a week	2	2
	2-3 times month	3	3
	Less often	4	4
	Never	5	5

65. A. Before (*worker's*) death, were there plans to send (any of) the child(ren) on to college?

Yes, was planning on it	1	62/0
Maybe, had thought about it	2	
No, no such plans	3	
Don't know	4	

B.   And how about now—are there (still) plans to send (any of) them to college?

Yes, attending now	1	63/0
Yes, planning to send	2	
Maybe, don't know yet	3	
No, no such plans	4	
Don't know	5	

C.   *If yes to A, but maybe or no to B:*
Why are there no longer plans to send (any of) them to college?

64/y

If no widow, end interview here.   Begin Deck 11

Ask Q's 66-74 of or about widow only.   _____

66. A.   Who did you (*widow*) rely on most for advice about handling the family financial matters after (*worker's*) death? Circle one under "A" below.

B.   Was there anybody else whose financial advice you relied on at that time? Code as many as apply under "B."

	A. Relied On Most		B. Also Relied On	
Family member (Specify)	1	7/R	1	8/R
Bank employee	2		2	
Company representative	3		3	
Union representative	4		4	
Physician	5		5	
Social agency (Specify)	6		6	
Clergyman	7		7	
Mortician or undertaker	8		8	
Attorney	9		9	
Insurance man	0		0	
Other (Specify)	X		X	
No one, or no one else	y		y	

67. Where would you (*widow*) go today if (you/she) needed advice about financial matters?

Same person as Q. 66	1	9/0
Someone else (Ask A & B)	2	
Don't know	3	

If someone else:
A. Who?

10/y

B. Why would (you/she) go to him instead of (*person named in Q. 66*)?

11/y

68. Before (*worker's*) death, did you (*widow*) belong to any groups, clubs, or organizations?

Yes (Ask A-C)	1	12/0
No	2	
Don't know	3	

If yes:
A. Which ones? Any others? Circle code "X" under "A" below next to each kind of group mentioned.

B. *Ask for each:* Would you say you were (she was) a very active member of (*group*), a fairly active member, or were you (was she) not very active in the group? Code under "B" below.

C. *Ask for each:* And how about today—are you (is she) very active in (*group*), fairly active, not active, or do you (does she) no longer belong to it? Code under "C" below.

Nature of Group	A. Member Of	B. Before Very Active	B. Before Fairly Active	B. Before Not Active		C. Today Very Active	C. Today Fairly Active	C. Today Not Active	C. Today No Longer Belong	
Religious or ethnic groups	X	1	2	3	13/0	1	2	3	4	14/0
Hobby, recreational, or social groups	X	1	2	3	15/0	1	2	3	4	16/0
Educational and cultural organizations (alumni organizations, PTA).	X	1	2	3	17/0	1	2	3	4	18/0
Civic or political groups (League of Women Voters)	X	1	2	3	19/0	1	2	3	4	20/0
Professional or other work-related groups	X	1	2	3	21/0	1	2	3	4	22/0
Other (SPECIFY)	X	1	2	3	23/0	1	2	3	4	24/0

69. Since (*worker's*) death, have you (has she) joined any (new) groups, or clubs, or organizations?

Yes (Ask A & B)	1	25/0
No	2	
Don't know	3	

If yes:

A. Which ones? Any others?

Religious or ethnic groups	1	26/0
Hobby, recreational, or social groups	2	
Educational and cultural organizations (alumni organizations, PTA)	3	
Civic or political groups (League of Women Voters)	4	
Professional or other work-related groups	5	
Other (Specify)	6	

B. How active would you say (you are/she is) in this (these)—very active, fairly active, or not active?

Very active	1	27/0
Fairly active	2	
Not active	3	

70. We are interested in how certain of your (*widow's*) activities may have changed since (*worker*) died. For example . . .

	More	Less	About Same	Don't Know	
A. Do you (Does she) watch television more now, or less, or about the same as before?	1	2	3	4	28/0
B. Do you (Does she) go to the movies more, or less, or about the same?	1	2	3	4	29/0
C. Do you (Does she) visit friends more, or less, or about the same?	1	2	3	4	30/0
D. How about inviting friends in to visit (you/her)?	1	2	3	4	31/0

If respondent is not widow, end interview here.

Ask Q's 71 and 72 only if respondent is widow *and* if one or more dependent children under 18 were living in worker's household at time of death (Q. 25, P. 8).

71. We all know that it's not often easy to raise a family, and that problems may come up which are difficult even for two parents to handle. In such cases, parents sometimes seek the help or advice of people outside the family.

   During the year or so before (*worker's*) death, did you or your husband ever turn to anyone for help or advice about your children?

Yes (Ask A-C)	1	32/0
No	2	

   If yes:
   A. Who did you turn to? Code as many as apply in column A. below.

	A.	C.		
	Source	Very Helpful	Fairly Helpful	No Help
Parents	1 33/0	1	2	3 34/0
Other relatives	2	1	2	3 35/0
Friends	3	1	2	3 36/0
A clergyman	4	1	2	3 37/0
A family counselor or social worker	5	1	2	3 38/0
A doctor	6	1	2	3 39/0
Teacher, school official	7	1	2	3 40/0
Anyone else (Specify)	8	1	2	3 41/0

   B. What sort of problems did you feel you needed help on?

   42/y

   C. Was (*source given in A*) very helpful to you, fairly helpful, or no real help at all? Circle appropriate code for each source in column C above.

72. And since (*worker's*) death, have you turned to anyone for help or advice about your children?

Yes (Ask A-C)	1	43/0
No	2	

If yes:

A. Who did you turn to? Code as many as apply in column A below.

	A.	C.		
	Source	Very Helpful	Fairly Helpful	No Help
Parents	1	1	2	3	45/0
Other relatives	2	1	2	3	46/0
Friends	3	1	2	3	47/0
A clergyman	4	1	2	3	48/0
A family counselor or social worker	5	1	2	3	49/0
A doctor	6	1	2	3	51/0
Teacher, school official	7	1	2	3	51/0
Anyone else (Specify)	8	1	2	3	52/0

B. What sort of problems did you feel you needed help on?

53/y

C. Was (*each source of help coded in Column A*) very helpful to you, fairly helpful, or no real help at all? Circle appropriate code for each source in column C above.

73. *Ask only if respondent is widow*

Did you ever at any (other) time seek help from a professional agency, like a marriage counselor or social welfare agency about some personal or family problem?

Yes (Ask A-C)	1	54/0
No	2	

If yes:

A. What group or agency was that?

55/y

B. Was that before or after your husband died?

Before	1	56/0
After	2	
Both	3	

C. Was (*source given in A*) very helpful to your, fairly helpful, or no real help at all?

Very helpful	1	57/0
Fairly helpful	2	
No help	3	

74. *Ask only of widows*

And lastly, I want to read you some statements about family benfits under Social Security, and you tell me whether they are true or false.

	True	False	Don't Know	
A. Social Security benefits to a surviving dependent are reduced if the dependent works and earns more than $1,500 during the year. Is that true or false?	1	2	3	58/0
B. If the mother works and earns more than $1,500 during the year, this does *not* affect the benefits of the surviving children under her care.	1	2	3	59/0
C. Generally, monthly payments will stop if the widow remarries.	1	2	3	60/0
D. Monthly payments will stop when a dependent child marries.	1	2	3	61/0
E. Monthly payments will stop when a dependent child reaches the age of 18, unless he is disabled.	1	2	3	62/0
F. Payments will stop if the surviving widow is less than 62 years of age and she no longer has in her care a child who is entitled to monthly payments.	1	2	3	63/0

Thank you very much. This has been a long interview and I hope I haven't tired you, but the information you've given me will be very helpful to other persons like yourself.

Time ended: ——— AM / PM   Total length of interview (minutes) ———

64-66/yyy

Answer these questions immediately after leaving respondent

A. In general, how cooperative was the respondent?
    Very cooperative   1   67/0
    Fairly cooperative   2
    Somewhat uncooperative   3
    Very uncooperative   4

B. Worker's race:
    White   1   68/0
    Black   2
    Other (Specify)   3

C. In general, how accurate do you feel the respondent's answers to the questions about income and expenditures are?
    Generally accurate   1   69/0
    OK with some exceptions
       (Answer D)   2
    Not very accurate
       (Answer D)   3

D. *If not generally accurate* What financial information is most likely to be inaccurate, as far as you could tell?

E. Did you or respondent use anyone else as an informant on any of these questions?
    Yes (Answer F & G)   1   70/0
    No   2

If yes:
F. Who? (Record name, address, and relationship to worker)

G. What information did this person supply?

H. Interviewer's signature:

G. What information did this person supply?

H. Interviewer's signature:

I. Date of interview:

Day 71-72/yy   Month   73/y

188

Q. 47   Supplement A

Workmen's Compensation

Worker's Name _____ ____   Case No. _____
                                                                    (1-4)

1. How much did you (*beneficiary*) receive as a funeral benefit from this
   source? $ _____ 5-8/yyy

2. Did you decide (Have you decided) to take the survivor's benefit as a lump
   sum or in installments?
                    Lump sum (Ask A)   1   9/0
                    Installments (Ask B-D)   2

   If lump sum:
   A. How much did (will) you recieve as a lump sum?
                                                $ _____ 10-14/yyyyy

   If Installments:
   B. How often (did/do/will) you receive installments?
                    Weekly   1   15/0
                    Monthly   2
                    Other (Specify)   3

   C. How much (did/do/will) you receive in each installment?
                                                $ _____ 16-18/yyy

   D. How long (did/do/will) the installments run altogether? Record number
       of weeks, months, *or* years.
                              _____ weeks   19-20/yy
                              _____ months   21-22/yy
                              _____ years   23-24/yy

                    Leave blank. Annual value of benefit:
                                                $ _____ 25-29/yyyyy

3. Did you know at the time that you had a choice between a lump-sum
   benefit and a weekly payment benefit?
                    Yes   1   30/0
                    No   2

4. A. If you had the decision to make over again, which form of benefit would you select now?

Lump sum	1	31/0
Weekly payment	2	
Don't know	3	

B. Why is that?

32/y

Q. 47   Supplement B

Public Liability

Worker's name _____ Case No. _____
(1-4)

1. Altogether, how much did (will) you receive from this source?

$ _____ 5-9/yyyyy

2. Did you have a choice between a lump-sum settlement and installment payments?

Yes (Ask A-C)	1	10/0
No (Ask D)	2	

If yes:
A. Which did you choose?

Lump sum	1	11/0
Installment payments	2	

B. If you had the decision to make over again, which form of benefit would you select now?

Lump sum	1	12/0
Installment payments	2	
Don't know	3	

C. Why is that?

13/y

If no:

D. If you had had a chance to choose, which form would you have selected?

Lump sum	1	14/0
Installment payments	2	
Don't know	3	

Q. 47   Supplement C

Veterans' Insurance

Worker's Name _____ Case No. _____

(1-4)

1. Did (Will) you (*beneficiary*) receive a funeral benefit from this source?

Yes (Ask A)	1	5/0
No	2	

   A. *If yes:* How much was that? $ _____ 6-9/yyyy

2. Did you decide (Have you decided) to take the survivor's benefit as a lump sum or in installments?

Lump sum (Ask A)	1	10/0
Installments (Ask B-D)	2	

If lump sum:

A. How much (did/will) you receive as a lump sum?

$ _____ 11-15/yyyyy

If installments:

B. How often (did/do/will) you receive installments?

Weekly	1	16/0
Monthly	2	
Other (Specify)	3	

C. How much (did/do/will) you receive in each installment?

$ _____ 17-19/yyy

D. How long (did/do/will) the installments run altogether? Record weeks, months, *or* years.

_____	weeks	20-21/yy
_____	months	22-23/yy
_____	years	24-25/yy

Leave blank. Annual value of benefit:

$ _____ 25-29/yyyyy

3. A. If you had the decision to make over again, which form of benefit would you select now?

Lump sum	1	30/0
Installment payments	2	
Don't know	3	

B. Why is that?

31/y

Q. 47 Supplement D

*Private Insurance, Fraternal Order Benefits, Travel
Accident Insurance, or Other Insurance*

Worker's Name _____ Case No. _____
(1-4)

1. How many (private insurance, fraternal order benefits, travel accident insurance, or other insurance) policies did (*worker*) have? If more than one,

This is "D" supplement ☐ of ☐
5/y   6/y

2. Was that (was the first one) a private insurance, fraternal order benefits, travel accident insurance, or what?

Private insurance	1	7/0
Fraternal order benefits	2	
Travel accident insurance	3	
Other (Specify)	4	

3. What kind of insurance was it?

Accident	1	8/0
Term life	2	
Ordinary life with cash value	3	
Endowment	4	
Other (Specify)	5	
Don't know	6	

4. How was the insurance premium paid—Was the money sent to the company, or did a company agent call to collect?

Money sent to company	1	9/0
Agent called to collect	2	
Don't know	3	

5. Did you receive a funeral (burial) benefit from this insurance?

Yes (Ask A)	1	10/0
No	2	

   A. *If yes:* How much did you receive as a funeral (burial) benefit?
   $ _____ 11-14/yyyy

6. Some insurance policies allow the beneficiaries a choice between taking the insurance payment in one lump sum or in monthly installments. Did this insurance company offer you this choice?

Yes	1	15/0
No	2	
Don't know	3	

7. Did you decide (Have you decided) to take the survivor's benefit as a lump sum or in installments?

Lump sum (Ask A)	1	16/0
Installments (Ask B-D)	2	

If lump sum:
A. How much did (will) you receive as a lump sum?
   $ _____ 17-21/yyyyy

If installments:
B. How often (did/do/will) you receive installments?

Weekly	1	22/0
Monthly	2	
Other (Specify)	3	

C. How much (did/do/will) you receive in each installment?
   $ _____ 23-25/yyy

D. How long (did/do/will) the installments run altogether? Record number of weeks, months, *or* years.

   _____ weeks 26-27/yy
   _____ months 28-29/yy
   _____ years 30-31/yy

Leave blank. Annual value of benefit:
   $ _____ 32-36/yyyyy

8. A. If you had a choice now between a lump-sum payment and installment payments, which one do you think you would select?

Lump sum	1	37/0
Installments	2	
Don't know	3	

    B. Why is that?

                                                      38/y

9. Did you receive any other benefits from this insurance, aside from money payments, such as a cemetery lot or grave marker?

Yes (Ask A & B)	1	39/0
No	2	

If yes:

    A. What was that? (What did you receive?)

                                                      40/y

    B. About how much money was this benefit worth to you?

                                       $ _____ 41-44/yyyy

Q. 47   Supplement E

Credit Union Life Insurance

Worker's Name _____ Case No. _____
                                                               (1-4)

1. How many credit union life insurance policies did (*worker*) have? If more than one, fill out supplement E for each.

                  This is "E" supplement   of
                                         5/y   6/y

2. What is the name of the Credit Union (with which he had the first policy)?

_____ 7/y

3. What kind of insurance was that?

Accident	1	8/0
Term life	2	
Ordinary life with cash value	3	
Endowment	4	
Other (Specify)	5	
Don't know	6	

4. Did you receive a funeral benefit from this source?

Yes (Ask A)	1	9/0
No	2	

   A. *If yes:* How much was that? $ _____ 10-13/yyyy

5. Did you decide (Have you decided) to take the survivor's benefit as a lump sum or in installments?

Lump sum (Ask A)	1	14/0
Installments (Ask B-D)	2	

If lump sum:
   A. How much did (will) you receive as a lump sum?

                                $ _____ 15-19/yyyyy

If installments:
   B. How often (did/do/will) you receive installments?

Weekly	1	20/0
Monthly	2	
Other (Specify)	3	

   C. How much (did/do/will) you receive in each installment?

                                  $ _____ 21-23/yyy

   D. How long (did/do/will) the installments run altogether? Record number of weeks, months, *or* years.

_____	weeks	24-25/yy
_____	months	26-27/yy
_____	years	28-29/yy

         Leave Blank. Annual value of benefit:

                                  $ _____ 30-34/yyyyy

6. A. If you had the decision to make over again, which form of benefit would you select now?

Lump sum	1	35/0
Installments	2	
Don't know	3	

   B. Why is that?

                                                 36/y

Notes

Notes

Chapter 2
Background, Aims, and Methodology

1. *Widows with Children Under Social Security,* Research Report Number 16, Social Security Administration, p. 1, the most recent study revealing such data.

2. *Statistical Abstract of the U.S.,* 1967, Table No. 406.

3. 1967, *Life Insurance Fact Book,* p. 10 and p. 37. Data on Life Insurance protection by occupation or income are not publicly available.

4. For a more comprehensive discussion of the role of society in providing for those in need see Edwin E. Witte, "Social Security: A Wild Dream or a Practical Plan?" *Social Security Perspectives,* ed. Robert J. Lampman (Madison, Wisconsin: The University of Wisconsin Press, 1962), Part I, pp. 3 and 4.

5. "City Worker's Family Budget," Bulletin 1570-1, U.S. Department of Labor, Bureau of Labor Statistics, Table 2.

6. The authors have depended heavily on the wage chronologies compiled and published by the Bureau of Labor Statistics and the UAW Research Dept. Specific sources are:

U.S. Bureau of Labor Statistics, *Wage Chronology: Ford Motor Company,* 1941-64, BLS Report No. 99, Revised 1965.

U.S. Bureau of Labor Statistics, *Wage Chronology: General Motors Corporation,* 1939-63, BLS Report No. 185, Revised 1964.

U.S. Bureau of Labor Statistics, *Wage Chronology: Chrysler Corporation,* 1939-64, BLS Report No. 198, Revised 1964.

7. Exhibits (A through E) to the Agreements of September 22, 1964 between the Chrysler Corporation and the UAW-AFL-CIO.

Agreements between UAW-AFL-CIO and the Ford Motor Company, Agreements dated November 23, 1964.

Supplemental Agreements Covering Pension Plan and Insurance Program, Exhibits A and B to Agreement between General Motors Corporation and the UAW-AFL-CIO dated October 5, 1964.

Chapter 5
Utilization of Group Life Insurance Proceeds

1. Jessica Mitford, *The American Way of Death* (New York; Simon and Schuster, 1963), p. 41.

2. Ruth Mulvey Harmer, *The High Cost of Dying* (New York; Collier Books, 1963), p. 9.

3. Abe Magrisso and Donald Rubin, "Death's High Toll," *I.U.D. Digest* (A quarterly publication of the Industrial Union Department, AFL-CIO), Fall, 1961, p. 69.

4. U.S., Congress, Senate, Subcommittee of the Committee on the Judiciary, *Antitrust Aspects of the Funeral Industry,* 89th Cong., 2d Sess., 1967, p. 20. Cited hereafter as Senate Subcommittee on Antitrust and Monopoly, *Antitrust Aspects of the Funeral Industry,* 1967.

5. Ibid.

6. Harmer, *High Cost of Dying,* p. 9.

7. U.S., Department of Commerce, Office of Business Economics, *Survey of Current Business,* Vol. 44, No. 7 (July 1964), 16.

Chapter 6
Personal Implications of the Breadwinner's Death

1. Murry Hausknecht, *The Joiners.* New York, the Bedminster Press, 1962.

Appendix B
Technical Notes on Methodology

1. For a discussion of sampling error of means and medians, see *Widows with Children under Social Security,* Research Report No. 16, U.S. Social Security Administration, P. 71.

About the Authors

Melvin A. Glasser was appointed Director of the Social Security Department, UAW, in 1963. He has also served as Secretary-Treasurer of the Michigan Health and Social Security Research Institue, Inc., since its founding in 1965. He came to the UAW from Brandeis University where he was Dean of University Resources and Visiting Professor at the Graduate School for Advanced Studies in Social Welfare. Mr. Glasser has worked extensively in the health and welfare fields in the U.S. and abroad and is the author of numerous articles in these fields. He is a past president of the International Federation of Social Workers and former Chairman of the Executive Committee of the National Health Council.

Eugene L. Loren is research consultant, Michigan Health and Social Security Research Institute, Inc., and research associate in the Social Security Department, UAW. He joined the UAW staff in 1967, after teaching labor economics and industrial relations at UCLA and Princeton University. He has served as a consultant to the Government of Malawi, the U.S. Bureau of Employment Security, and the U.S. Office of Economic Opportunity. He is a member of the American Economic Association and the Industrial Relations Research Association and an associate member of the Michigan Actuarial Society.

Willard E. Solenberger is research consultant, Michigan Health and Social Security Research Institute, Inc., and Assistant Director of the Social Security Department, UAW. He joined the UAW staff in 1949 following earlier work in the welfare and social insurance fields. He has been closely associated with the development and collective bargaining of UAW pension, group insurance and unemployment benefit plans in the U.S. and Canada. Mr. Solenberger is a member of the American Pension Conference and an associate member of the Michigan Actuarial Society. He has presented papers at numerous national and regional pension and insurance conferences.

DATE DUE